LIVING LITURGY™

for Music Ministers

Year A • 2020

Brian Schmisek
Katy Beedle Rice
Diana Macalintal

LITURGICAL PRESS
Collegeville, Minnesota

www.litpress.org

Presented to

_____

in grateful appreciation
for your music ministry

_____

_____
(date)

USING THIS RESOURCE

Living Liturgy for Music Ministers™ is a resource intended to assist music ministers in their preparation for the liturgy on Sundays and selected solemnities, as well as Ash Wednesday. Included here are reflections on the gospel, and some insight into how the word of God informs daily life. It is hoped that the commentaries and reflections in this resource will assist music ministers with their own personal encounter with the sacred text. Music ministers who have a better understanding of the readings may be more apt to sing with a greater sensitivity to the deeper meaning of God's word.

Living Liturgy for Music Ministers™ has reflections on the gospel readings, brief commentaries connecting the responsorial psalm to the readings, followed by reflections to assist psalmists with preparing for proclamation of the psalms. There are prayers provided for musicians to use with their own spiritual preparation for their ministry. Also included are the readings and responsorial psalms for every Sunday of the liturgical year, as well as for certain solemnities and Ash Wednesday. The second readings are found in an appendix.

This book is an essential resource for music ministers whose own spirituality is nourished by the liturgical cycle and the accompanying Scripture readings, especially the gospel and the psalm. The following outline suggests how this resource might be used by music ministers as they prepare for the liturgical assembly. Of course, adaptations are encouraged as there is no one "right" way to use this book.

On Monday, read only the gospel and reflect on it. Then, read "Reflecting on Living the Gospel" before reading the gospel again. What new insights come to mind? How does the reflection inform your understanding of the sacred text?

On Tuesday, read the first reading. What connections, if any, do you find between it and the gospel? This is a good time to read "Connecting the Responsorial Psalm to the Readings." What new insights come to mind for you? How do these readings inform the situation at your parish, or with your fellow music ministers?

On Wednesday, read the psalm in a prayerful manner. What connections do you draw between the psalm, the gospel, and the first reading? If it is helpful, read the second reading too and let the Scriptures percolate in your spiritual life, with insights bubbling up naturally. When we have been reading God's word, these insights happen not only in prayer but also throughout the week at home, at work, and in daily life.

On Thursday, spend some time with "Psalmist Preparation." How will you allow some of the spiritual insights you've gained through prayer to inform your proclamation of the psalm?

On Friday, if you haven't already been singing the psalm with your accompanist or fellow ministers, now is a good time to start, at least on your own, or *a cappella*. Use the "Prayer" together as a group or pray it on your own either before or after your practice.

On Saturday and Sunday, spend time in quiet prayer, allowing yourself to be an instrument in God's hands so that the gathered assembly might find meaning and spiritual insight through your ministry. In your prayer allow words or phrases from the gospel, psalm, and first and second readings to come to mind.

Many music ministers find this to be a rich ministry, filled with spirituality and giving new meaning to their daily lives. The personal encounter with the living and sacred text, being the vehicle through which the assembly hears God's word, and the fellowship one experiences throughout the week are sources of consolation and joy. When we minister with the gifts given to us by God, we become who we are meant to be. We actualize the charisms God has bestowed on us, not for our sakes alone, but for the building up of the Christian community. In this way, music ministers live their Christian baptism.

Gospel (Matt 24:37-44; L I A)

Jesus said to his disciples: "As it was in the days of Noah, so it will be at the coming of the Son of Man. In those days before the flood, they were eating and drinking, marrying and giving in marriage, up to the day that Noah entered the ark. They did not know until the flood came and carried them all away. So will it be also at the coming of the Son of Man. Two men will be out in  the field; one will be taken, and one will be left. Two women will be grinding at the mill; one will be taken, and one will be left. Therefore, stay awake! For you do not know on which day your Lord will come. Be sure of this: if the master of the house had known the hour of night when the thief was coming, he would have stayed awake and not let his house be broken into. So too, you also must be prepared, for at an hour you do not expect, the Son of Man will come."

First Reading (Isa 2:1-5)

This is what Isaiah, son of Amoz,
  saw concerning Judah and Jerusalem.
    In days to come,
  the mountain of the LORD's house
    shall be established as the highest mountain
    and raised above the hills.
All nations shall stream toward it;
  many peoples shall come and say:
"Come, let us climb the LORD's mountain,
  to the house of the God of Jacob,
that he may instruct us in his ways,
  and we may walk in his paths."
For from Zion shall go forth instruction,
  and the word of the LORD from Jerusalem.
He shall judge between the nations,
  and impose terms on many peoples.
They shall beat their swords into plowshares
  and their spears into pruning hooks;

one nation shall not raise the sword against another,
nor shall they train for war again.
O house of Jacob, come,
let us walk in the light of the LORD!

Responsorial Psalm (Ps 122:1-2, 3-4, 4-5, 6-7, 8-9)

R℣. Let us go rejoicing to the house of the Lord.

I rejoiced because they said to me,
"We will go up to the house of the LORD."
And now we have set foot
within your gates, O Jerusalem.

R℣. Let us go rejoicing to the house of the Lord.

Jerusalem, built as a city
with compact unity.
To it the tribes go up,
the tribes of the LORD.

R℣. Let us go rejoicing to the house of the Lord.

According to the decree for Israel,
to give thanks to the name of the LORD.
In it are set up judgment seats,
seats for the house of David.

R℣. Let us go rejoicing to the house of the Lord.

Pray for the peace of Jerusalem!
May those who love you prosper!
May peace be within your walls,
prosperity in your buildings.

R℣. Let us go rejoicing to the house of the Lord.

Because of my brothers and friends
I will say, "Peace be within you!"
Because of the house of the LORD, our God,
I will pray for your good.

R℣. Let us go rejoicing to the house of the Lord.

See Appendix, p. 200, for Second Reading

Reflecting on Living the Gospel

We are not complacent. The mystery of Christianity, the life, death, resurrection, and ongoing life of Jesus animates us. Any tendency to become lethargic is thwarted by a resounding call to "stay awake!" We are not carried away by a glittering spectacle. Our life in Christ makes us rooted in God's vision of the world. We see the world through new lenses. We are prepared for anything that might come. In a state of preparation, then, we are alert, aware, and awake. The metamorphosis on the horizon approaches. It is coming, though we know not when.

Connecting the Responsorial Psalm to the Readings

In the first reading, the prophet Isaiah foresees a time when the temple in Jerusalem ("the mountain of the Lord's house") shall not only belong to God's chosen people, but to all the peoples of the world. For "[a]ll nations shall stream toward it" in search of divine wisdom and guidance. Our psalm tells us why the temple, "the house of the Lord," has the ability to attract all the peoples of the world—this is a house of joy, one that promises unity, a place of peace and justice, and what nation doesn't long for these things?

Psalmist Preparation

We have entered into the time of Advent, and although we might associate the color purple with a time of penance, fasting, and preparation, we are called to joyfully journey toward the feast of Christmas and the fullness of the kingdom of God. The responsorial psalm calls us to "go rejoicing to the house of the Lord." Is your parish a place that elicits joy?

Prayer

God of new beginnings,
we give thanks that we may stand within your gates
and rejoice in your holy temple.
May your peace dwell with us always.
Show us, Lord, your love,
and grant us your salvation. Amen.

Gospel (Matt 3:1-12; L4A)

John the Baptist appeared, preaching in
the desert of Judea and saying, "Repent,
for the kingdom of heaven is at hand!"
It was of him that the prophet Isaiah
had spoken when he said:

> *A voice of one crying out in*
>   *the desert,*
> *Prepare the way of the Lord,*
>   *make straight his paths.*

John wore clothing made of camel's hair and had a leather belt around
his waist. His food was locusts and wild honey. At that time Jerusalem,
all Judea, and the whole region around the Jordan were going out to him
and were being baptized by him in the Jordan River as they acknowl-
edged their sins.

When he saw many of the Pharisees and Sadducees coming to his
baptism, he said to them, "You brood of vipers! Who warned you to flee
from the coming wrath? Produce good fruit as evidence of your repentance. And do not presume to say to yourselves, 'We have Abraham as
our father.' For I tell you, God can raise up children to Abraham from
these stones. Even now the ax lies at the root of the trees. Therefore
every tree that does not bear good fruit will be cut down and thrown into
the fire. I am baptizing you with water, for repentance, but the one who
is coming after me is mightier than I. I am not worthy to carry his sandals. He will baptize you with the Holy Spirit and fire. His winnowing
fan is in his hand. He will clear his threshing floor and gather his wheat
into his barn, but the chaff he will burn with unquenchable fire."

First Reading (Isa 11:1-10)

> On that day, a shoot shall sprout from the stump of Jesse,
>   and from his roots a bud shall blossom.
> The spirit of the Lord shall rest upon him:
>   a spirit of wisdom and of understanding,
> a spirit of counsel and of strength,
>   a spirit of knowledge and of fear of the Lord,
>   and his delight shall be the fear of the Lord.
> Not by appearance shall he judge,
>   nor by hearsay shall he decide,

but he shall judge the poor with justice,
and decide aright for the land's afflicted.
He shall strike the ruthless with the rod of his mouth,
and with the breath of his lips he shall slay the wicked.
Justice shall be the band around his waist,
and faithfulness a belt upon his hips.
Then the wolf shall be a guest of the lamb,
and the leopard shall lie down with the kid;
the calf and the young lion shall browse together,
with a little child to guide them.
The cow and the bear shall be neighbors,
together their young shall rest;
the lion shall eat hay like the ox.
The baby shall play by the cobra's den,
and the child lay his hand on the adder's lair.
There shall be no harm or ruin on all my holy mountain;
for the earth shall be filled with knowledge of the Lord,
as water covers the sea.
On that day, the root of Jesse,
set up as a signal for the nations,
the Gentiles shall seek out,
for his dwelling shall be glorious.

Responsorial Psalm (Ps 72:1-2, 7-8, 12-13, 17)

℟. (cf. 7) Justice shall flourish in his time, and fullness of peace for ever.

O God, with your judgment endow the king,
and with your justice, the king's son;
he shall govern your people with justice
and your afflicted ones with judgment.

℟. Justice shall flourish in his time, and fullness of peace for ever.

Justice shall flower in his days,
and profound peace, till the moon be no more.
May he rule from sea to sea,
and from the River to the ends of the earth.

℟. Justice shall flourish in his time, and fullness of peace for ever.

For he shall rescue the poor when he cries out,
   and the afflicted when he has no one to help him.
He shall have pity for the lowly and the poor;
   the lives of the poor he shall save.
℞. Justice shall flourish in his time, and fullness of peace for ever.

May his name be blessed forever;
   as long as the sun his name shall remain.
In him shall all the tribes of the earth be blessed;
   all the nations shall proclaim his happiness.
℞. Justice shall flourish in his time, and fullness of peace for ever.

See Appendix, p. 200, for Second Reading

Reflecting on Living the Gospel

As human beings we desire consistency, predictability, and stability.
Though it's good to experience new things, not many of us thrive on
doing new things all the time. Our lives may be punctuated by difference,
but regularity reigns. Even so, it's good for us to be shaken up a bit and
jostled from our regular routine, as John the Baptist is doing today. We
are reminded that we need to repent, turn away from selfish interests
and turn toward God. What regular routines do we need to abandon?
From what in our lives do we need to turn away? An interior reorienta-
tion toward God and the values of his kingdom is demanded.

Connecting the Responsorial Psalm to the Readings

Our responsorial psalm paints us a picture of the kingdom of God: "Justice shall flourish in his time, and fullness of peace forever." In the first
reading Isaiah prophesies that the one to come shall have justice as "the
band around his waist." This justice is the force that hears the cries of
the poor and bears good fruit in the lives of those who live by its dic-
tates. The harsh words John the Baptist has for the Pharisees and the
Sadducees is a warning for anyone in a position of religious leadership.
Later in Matthew's gospel, Jesus will describe the principal fault of these
religious leaders by stating, "They tie up heavy burdens [hard to carry]
and lay them on people's shoulders, but they will not lift a finger to move
them" (23:4; NABRE).

Psalmist Preparation

What enables you, as ministers who lead the people of God in worship and song, to minister from a place of humility, formed by justice and peace?

Prayer

God of all nations, you chose John the Baptist
to be your voice in the desert.
May our voices join with his to announce that your salvation is near.
Justice shall flourish in his time,
and fullness of peace forever. Amen.

DECEMBER 9, 2019

Gospel (Luke 1:26-38; L689)

The angel Gabriel was sent from God to a town of Galilee called Nazareth, to a virgin betrothed to a man named Joseph, of the house of David, and the virgin's name was Mary. And coming to her, he said, "Hail, full of grace! The Lord is with you." But she was greatly troubled at what was said and pondered what sort of greeting this might be. Then the angel said to her, "Do not be afraid, Mary, for you have found favor with God. Behold, you will conceive in your womb and bear a son, and you shall name him Jesus. He will be great and will be called Son of the Most High, and the Lord God will give him the throne of David his father, and he will rule over the house of Jacob forever, and of his Kingdom there will be no end." But Mary said to the angel, "How can this be, since I have no relations with a man?" And the angel said to her in reply, "The Holy Spirit will come upon you, and the power of the Most High will overshadow you. Therefore the child to be born will be called holy, the Son of God. And behold, Elizabeth, your relative, has also conceived a son in her old age, and this is the sixth month for her who was called barren; for nothing will be impossible for God." Mary said, "Behold, I am the handmaid of the Lord. May it be done to me according to your word." Then the angel departed from her.

First Reading (Gen 3:9-15, 20)

After the man, Adam, had eaten of the tree, the LORD God called to the man and asked him, "Where are you?" He answered, "I heard you in the garden; but I was afraid, because I was naked, so I hid myself." Then he asked, "Who told you that you were naked? You have eaten, then, from the tree of which I had forbidden you to eat!" The man replied, "The woman whom you put here with me— she gave me fruit from the tree, and so I ate it." The LORD God then asked the woman, "Why did you do such a thing?" The woman answered, "The serpent tricked me into it, so I ate it."

Then the LORD God said to the serpent:

"Because you have done this, you shall be banned
    from all the animals
    and from all the wild creatures;
on your belly shall you crawl,
    and dirt shall you eat
    all the days of your life.
I will put enmity between you and the woman,
    and between your offspring and hers;
he will strike at your head,
    while you strike at his heel."

The man called his wife Eve, because she became the mother of all the living.

Responsorial Psalm (Ps 98:1, 2-3, 3-4)

R℣. (1a) Sing to the Lord a new song, for he has done marvelous deeds.

Sing to the LORD a new song,
    for he has done wondrous deeds;
his right hand has won victory for him,
    his holy arm.

R℣. Sing to the Lord a new song, for he has done marvelous deeds.

The LORD has made his salvation known:
    in the sight of the nations he has revealed his justice.
He has remembered his kindness and his faithfulness
    toward the house of Israel.

R℣. Sing to the Lord a new song, for he has done marvelous deeds.

All the ends of the earth have seen
    the salvation by our God.
Sing joyfully to the LORD, all you lands;
    break into song; sing praise.

R℣. Sing to the Lord a new song, for he has done marvelous deeds.

See Appendix, p. 200, for Second Reading

Reflecting on Living the Gospel

Luke's story of the annunciation, not the immaculate conception, is our gospel reading. Nowhere in the Scriptures do we have an account of Mary being conceived, and so there is no account of her being conceived without sin, which is the feast we celebrate today. Instead, in the Gospel of Luke we have the news announced to Mary by an angel that she was to be the mother of Jesus. And we celebrate today the Immaculate Conception, the purity of Mary from the moment she herself was conceived. The theological mysteries we proclaim are worthy of reflection, thought, prayer, and conversation with other Christians.

Connecting the Responsorial Psalm to the Readings

The responsorial psalm for today joyfully encourages us to "Sing to the Lord a new song, for he has done marvelous deeds." In our gospel reading from Luke, a new moment in salvation history is ushered in—the era of our redemption through God becoming incarnate in the womb of the Virgin Mary. The song of Mary's life takes on a new key from this moment forward; she bears Christ to the world and then points to him continuously throughout her life, telling us, "Do whatever he tells you" (John 2:5; NABRE).

Psalmist Preparation

The sublime mystery of God become flesh to dwell among us is one we can never fully unpack. It calls us to constantly sing a new song to our God as we experience life in Christ. Where is God calling you to newness right now?

Prayer

Prepared from birth to trust in you,
Mary believed in your Word, O God.
May we share her faith that all things are possible with you.
Sing to the Lord a new song,
for God has done marvelous deeds. Amen.

Gospel (Matt 11:2-11; L7A)

When John the Baptist heard in prison of the works of the Christ, he sent his disciples to Jesus with this question, "Are you the one who is to come, or should we look for another?" Jesus said to them in reply, "Go and tell John what you hear and see: the blind regain their sight, the lame walk, lepers are cleansed, the deaf hear, the dead are raised, and the poor have the good news proclaimed to them. And blessed is the one who takes no offense at me."

As they were going off, Jesus began to speak to the crowds about John, "What did you go out to the desert to see? A reed swayed by the wind? Then what did you go out to see? Someone dressed in fine clothing? Those who wear fine clothing are in royal palaces. Then why did you go out? To see a prophet? Yes, I tell you, and more than a prophet. This is the one about whom it is written:

Behold, I am sending my messenger ahead of you;
he will prepare your way before you.

Amen, I say to you, among those born of women there has been none greater than John the Baptist; yet the least in the kingdom of heaven is greater than he."

First Reading (Isa 35:1-6a, 10)

The desert and the parched land will exult;
    the steppe will rejoice and bloom.
They will bloom with abundant flowers,
    and rejoice with joyful song.
The glory of Lebanon will be given to them,
    the splendor of Carmel and Sharon;
they will see the glory of the LORD,
    the splendor of our God.
Strengthen the hands that are feeble,
    make firm the knees that are weak,
say to those whose hearts are frightened:
    Be strong, fear not!

Here is your God,
    he comes with vindication;
with divine recompense
    he comes to save you.
Then will the eyes of the blind be opened,
    the ears of the deaf be cleared;
then will the lame leap like a stag,
    then the tongue of the mute will sing.

Those whom the LORD has ransomed will return
    and enter Zion singing,
    crowned with everlasting joy;
they will meet with joy and gladness,
    sorrow and mourning will flee.

Responsorial Psalm (Ps 146:6-7, 8-9, 9-10)

℟. (cf. Isaiah 35:4) Lord, come and save us. *or:* ℟. Alleluia.

The LORD God keeps faith forever,
    secures justice for the oppressed,
    gives food to the hungry.
The LORD sets captives free.

℟. Lord, come and save us. *or:* ℟. Alleluia.

The LORD gives sight to the blind;
    the LORD raises up those who were bowed down.
The LORD loves the just;
    the LORD protects strangers.

℟. Lord, come and save us. *or:* ℟. Alleluia.

The fatherless and the widow he sustains,
    but the way of the wicked he thwarts.
The LORD shall reign forever;
    your God, O Zion, through all generations.

℟. Lord, come and save us. *or:* ℟. Alleluia.

See Appendix, p. 200, for Second Reading

Reflecting on Living the Gospel

Today we learn about John the Baptist's expectations for Jesus. John was likely offended at Jesus' behavior and preaching because it was not what he had foretold. The disconnect was so great that John wondered if there was someone else who was to come. This is a good reminder for us to temper our expectations of others. We are ultimately responsible for ourselves, not anyone else. We can let God raise up in others the special gifts, talents, and abilities given to them. We would do well to abandon any desire to control others through the expectations we might place on them.

Connecting the Responsorial Psalm to the Readings

Today's psalm gives us a litany of the Lord's saving actions that mirror closely the words of Jesus to John's disciples and the proclamation of the prophet Isaiah to the people of Israel: "Here is your God, / he comes with vindication; / with divine recompense / he comes to save you." The psalmist names God as the one who feeds the hungry, frees captives, protects the vulnerable, and in all ways, "raises up those who [are] bowed down." These are the markers of discernment that Jesus points to for John's disciples on their quest to discover if he is the one they have been waiting for. Jesus' saving actions reveal him to be the incarnate Son of the living God, who has been the champion of his people throughout history.

Psalmist Preparation

This week, take time each evening to pause and consider where throughout the day you have encountered the saving action of God who "keeps faith forever."

Prayer

The signs of your glory, O God, are all around us
in the blind who see, the deaf who hear, and the dead raised to new life.
May our song announce glad tidings to all in need.
The Lord shall reign forever,
the Lord who comes to save us. Amen.

DECEMBER 22, 2019

Gospel (Matt 1:18-24; L10A)

This is how the birth of Jesus Christ came about. When his mother Mary was betrothed to Joseph, but before they lived together, she was found with child through the Holy Spirit. Joseph her husband, since he was a righteous man, yet unwilling to expose her to shame, decided to divorce her quietly. Such was his intention when, behold, the angel of the Lord appeared to him in a dream and said, "Joseph, son of

David, do not be afraid to take Mary your wife into your home. For it is through the Holy Spirit that this child has been conceived in her. She will bear a son and you are to name him Jesus, because he will save his people from their sins." All this took place to fulfill what the Lord had said through the prophet:

> *Behold, the virgin shall conceive and bear a son,*
> *and they shall name him Emmanuel,*

which means "God is with us." When Joseph awoke, he did as the angel of the Lord had commanded him and took his wife into his home.

First Reading (Isa 7:10-14)

The LORD spoke to Ahaz, saying: Ask for a sign from the LORD, your God; let it be deep as the netherworld, or high as the sky! But Ahaz answered, "I will not ask! I will not tempt the LORD!" Then Isaiah said: Listen, O house of David! Is it not enough for you to weary people, must you also weary my God? Therefore the Lord himself will give you this sign: the virgin shall conceive, and bear a son, and shall name him Emmanuel.

Responsorial Psalm (Ps 24:1-2, 3-4, 5-6)

℟. (7c and 10b) Let the Lord enter; he is king of glory.

The LORD's are the earth and its fullness;
    the world and those who dwell in it.
For he founded it upon the seas
    and established it upon the rivers.

℟. Let the Lord enter; he is king of glory.

Who can ascend the mountain of the LORD?
 or who may stand in his holy place?
One whose hands are sinless, whose heart is clean,
 who desires not what is vain.

℟. Let the Lord enter; he is king of glory.

He shall receive a blessing from the LORD,
 a reward from God his savior.
Such is the race that seeks for him,
 that seeks the face of the God of Jacob.

℟. Let the Lord enter; he is king of glory.

See Appendix, p. 201, for Second Reading

Reflecting on Living the Gospel

"Ready or not, here we come" seems an appropriate phrase for this
Fourth Sunday of Advent. Christmas will be here soon whether we are
ready or not. And as Christmas is the celebration of the birth of a child,
this phrase is appropriate for that too. Many parents reach a sometimes
startling conclusion that the baby will be here whether they are ready or
not. No matter how much preparation we've done this Advent, there's
likely more we could do. The Christ Child is about to be born. Life has
profound meaning. Ready or not, Christmas is coming.

Connecting the Responsorial Psalm to the Readings

Today's responsorial psalm proclaims, "Let the Lord enter; he is king of
glory." This psalm is sung to the one who created the earth and sky, who
"founded" the oceans and "established" the rivers. And yet, we also sing
this hymn to the child of Bethlehem, growing within his mother's womb,
vulnerable to the perceptions of a society that sees him as something
shameful, a baby conceived out of wedlock.

Psalmist Preparation

The three figures in today's readings (Ahaz, king of Judah; Paul, "a slave
of Christ Jesus"; and Joseph, the husband of Mary) are invited to have
radical trust in the Lord. From resisting the protection offered by a
powerful nation, to proclaiming Jesus Christ in hostile territory and fos-
tering a child not his own, these men are asked to reject the safe choice

and instead trust in the God of the unexpected. Where is God asking for this trust in your life?

Prayer

Your name, Emmanuel, is your promise that we are not alone.
Help us be more like Joseph that we may never fear
to open our homes and our hearts to your presence.
Let the Lord enter
for he is the king of glory. Amen.

Gospel (Matt 1:1-25
[or Matt 1:18-25]; L13 ABC)

The book of the genealogy of
Jesus Christ, the son of David, the
son of Abraham.

Abraham became the father of
Isaac, Isaac the father of Jacob,
Jacob the father of Judah and his
brothers. Judah became the father
of Perez and Zerah, whose mother
was Tamar. Perez became the father of Hezron, Hezron the father of
Ram, Ram the father of Amminadab. Amminadab became the father of
Nahshon, Nahshon the father of Salmon, Salmon the father of Boaz,
whose mother was Rahab. Boaz became the father of Obed, whose
mother was Ruth. Obed became the father of Jesse, Jesse the father of
David the king.

David became the father of Solomon, whose mother had been the wife
of Uriah. Solomon became the father of Rehoboam, Rehoboam the father
of Abijah, Abijah the father of Asaph. Asaph became the father of
Jehoshaphat, Jehoshaphat the father of Joram, Joram the father of Uzziah.
Uzziah became the father of Jotham, Jotham the father of Ahaz, Ahaz the
father of Hezekiah. Hezekiah became the father of Manasseh, Manasseh
the father of Amos, Amos the father of Josiah. Josiah became the father
of Jechoniah and his brothers at the time of the Babylonian exile.

After the Babylonian exile, Jechoniah became the father of Shealtiel,
Shealtiel the father of Zerubbabel, Zerubbabel the father of Abiud. Abiud
became the father of Eliakim, Eliakim the father of Azor, Azor the father
of Zadok. Zadok became the father of Achim, Achim the father of Eliud,
Eliud the father of Eleazar. Eleazar became the father of Matthan,
Matthan the father of Jacob, Jacob the father of Joseph, the husband of
Mary. Of her was born Jesus who is called the Christ.

Thus the total number of generations from Abraham to David is fourteen generations; from David to the Babylonian exile, fourteen generations; from the Babylonian exile to the Christ, fourteen generations.

Now this is how the birth of Jesus Christ came about. When his mother
Mary was betrothed to Joseph, but before they lived together, she was
found with child through the Holy Spirit. Joseph her husband, since he was
a righteous man, yet unwilling to expose her to shame, decided to divorce

her quietly. Such was his intention when, behold, the angel of the Lord appeared to him in a dream and said, "Joseph, son of David, do not be afraid to take Mary your wife into your home. For it is through the Holy Spirit that this child has been conceived in her. She will bear a son and you are to name him Jesus, because he will save his people from their sins." All this took place to fulfill what the Lord had said through the prophet:

Behold, the virgin shall conceive and bear a son,
and they shall name him Emmanuel,

which means "God is with us." When Joseph awoke, he did as the angel of the Lord had commanded him and took his wife into his home. He had no relations with her until she bore a son, and he named him Jesus.

First Reading (Isa 62:1-5)

For Zion's sake I will not be silent,
for Jerusalem's sake I will not be quiet,
until her vindication shines forth like the dawn
and her victory like a burning torch.

Nations shall behold your vindication,
and all the kings your glory;
you shall be called by a new name
pronounced by the mouth of the LORD.
You shall be a glorious crown in the hand of the LORD,
a royal diadem held by your God.
No more shall people call you "Forsaken,"
or your land "Desolate,"
but you shall be called "My Delight,"
and your land "Espoused."
For the LORD delights in you
and makes your land his spouse.
As a young man marries a virgin,
your Builder shall marry you;
and as a bridegroom rejoices in his bride
so shall your God rejoice in you.

Responsorial Psalm (Ps 89:4-5, 16-17, 27, 29)

R̸. (2a) For ever I will sing the goodness of the Lord.

I have made a covenant with my chosen one,
    I have sworn to David my servant:
forever will I confirm your posterity
    and establish your throne for all generations.

R̸. For ever I will sing the goodness of the Lord.

Blessed the people who know the joyful shout;
    in the light of your countenance, O LORD, they walk.
At your name they rejoice all the day,
    and through your justice they are exalted.

R̸. For ever I will sing the goodness of the Lord.

He shall say of me, "You are my father,
    my God, the Rock, my savior."
Forever I will maintain my kindness toward him,
    and my covenant with him stands firm.

R̸. For ever I will sing the goodness of the Lord.

See Appendix, p. 201, for Second Reading

Reflecting on Living the Gospel

The first part of the gospel reading is the genealogy of Jesus. The list of names can seem long, especially when we're anticipating the joys of Christmas. And yet, each year, these names are read aloud on this night for a reason. Within the family tree of Jesus we find some shocking ancestors. Non-Jews, adulterers, and others of questionable moral character are named alongside great patriarchs and matriarchs, and heroes and heroines of Israel's past. And the last name in the list is "Jesus, who is called the Christ." The angel tells Joseph, "[Y]ou are to name him Jesus, / because he will save his people from their sins."

Connecting the Responsorial Psalm to the Readings

The psalmist proclaims, "Blessed the people who know the joyful shout; / in the light of your countenance, O LORD, they walk." In the first reading, the prophet Isaiah reminds the people of Israel of their blessedness during a dark time in the nation's history. Although the Babylonian exile has ended and the people are returning to Israel, the work of rebuilding is difficult. And yet the prophet promises, "No more shall people call you 'Forsaken,' / or your land 'Desolate,' / but you shall be called 'My Delight.'"

Psalmist Preparation
God's covenant with his people remains strong in times of darkness and in the joy of the light. This night we celebrate our redemption come in the form of a baby who is true God and true man and who "will save his people from their sins." May our own joyful shout come from the sure knowledge that we are counted among God's people.

Prayer
In every age, through sinner and saint,
in our darkest nights and days of peace,
you have made us, Lord, your lineage of grace.
For this may we never be silent.
For ever let us sing of your goodness, O God. Amen.

Gospel (Luke 2:1-14; L14ABC)

In those days a decree went out from Caesar Augustus that the whole world should be enrolled. This was the first enrollment, when Quirinius was governor of Syria. So all went to be enrolled, each to his own town. And Joseph too went up from Galilee from the town of Nazareth to Judea, to the city of David that is called Bethlehem, because he was of the house and family of David, to be enrolled with Mary, his betrothed, who was with child. While they were there, the time came for her to have her child, and she gave birth to her firstborn son. She wrapped him in swaddling clothes and laid him in a manger, because there was no room for them in the inn.

Now there were shepherds in that region living in the fields and keeping the night watch over their flock. The angel of the Lord appeared to them and the glory of the Lord shone around them, and they were struck with great fear. The angel said to them, "Do not be afraid; for behold, I proclaim to you good news of great joy that will be for all the people. For today in the city of David a savior has been born for you who is Christ and Lord. And this will be a sign for you: you will find an infant wrapped in swaddling clothes and lying in a manger." And suddenly there was a multitude of the heavenly host with the angel, praising God and saying:

"Glory to God in the highest
and on earth peace to those on whom his favor rests."

First Reading (Isa 9:1-6)

The people who walked in darkness
have seen a great light;
upon those who dwelt in the land of gloom
a light has shone.
You have brought them abundant joy
and great rejoicing,
as they rejoice before you as at the harvest,
as people make merry when dividing spoils.
For the yoke that burdened them,
the pole on their shoulder,

and the rod of their taskmaster
>you have smashed, as on the day of Midian.
For every boot that tramped in battle,
>every cloak rolled in blood,
>will be burned as fuel for flames.
For a child is born to us, a son is given us;
>upon his shoulder dominion rests.
They name him Wonder-Counselor, God-Hero,
>Father-Forever, Prince of Peace.
His dominion is vast
>and forever peaceful,
from David's throne, and over his kingdom,
>which he confirms and sustains
by judgment and justice,
>both now and forever.
The zeal of the LORD of hosts will do this!

Responsorial Psalm (Ps 96:1-2, 2-3, 11-12, 13)

R̪. (Luke 2:11) Today is born our Savior, Christ the Lord.

Sing to the LORD a new song;
>sing to the LORD, all you lands.
Sing to the LORD; bless his name.

R̪. Today is born our Savior, Christ the Lord.

Announce his salvation, day after day.
>Tell his glory among the nations;
>among all peoples, his wondrous deeds.

R̪. Today is born our Savior, Christ the Lord.

Let the heavens be glad and the earth rejoice;
>let the sea and what fills it resound;
>let the plains be joyful and all that is in them!
Then shall all the trees of the forest exult.

R̪. Today is born our Savior, Christ the Lord.

They shall exult before the LORD, for he comes;
>for he comes to rule the earth.
He shall rule the world with justice
>and the peoples with his constancy.

R̪. Today is born our Savior, Christ the Lord.

THE NATIVITY OF THE LORD
Mass at Midnight

See Appendix, p. 201, for Second Reading

Reflecting on Living the Gospel
Midnight by definition is a time of darkness, the middle of the night. And yet, it is during this time that light enters the world by the birth of the Christ, the Savior. Such a stark contrast is not by accident in the Gospel of Luke or in our liturgy tonight. We recall how God brings life from death, joy from sadness, and light from darkness. When we face moments of darkness in our own lives, let us recall the Christian faith that is at our core, that sees the birth of a child during the night watch as a profound moment of grace.

Connecting the Responsorial Psalm to the Readings
The responsorial psalm proclaims, "Today is born our Savior, Christ the Lord." In the first reading from the prophet Isaiah, we are given the names for this Savior, this child born to us, "Wonder-Counselor, God-Hero, / Father-Forever, Prince of Peace." In the gospel, the angel of the Lord tells the astonished shepherds that this Savior, this child of many names, is "for all the people."

Psalmist Preparation
On this holy night, as you lead the assembly in proclaiming that their savior has been born, consider how you know this savior today in your own life. Which name for Jesus (Wonder-Counselor, God-Hero, Father-Forever, Prince of Peace) captivates your imagination? How are you being called to meet this savior anew?

Prayer
Wonder-Counselor, you guide us in right paths:
Glory to God in the highest!
God-Hero, you fill us with hope:
Glory to God in the highest!
Father-Forever, you never abandon us:
Glory to God in the highest!
Prince of Peace, you dispel our darkness:
Glory to God in the highest! Amen.

DECEMBER 25, 2019

Gospel (Luke 2:15-20; L15ABC)

When the angels went away from them to heaven, the shepherds said to one another, "Let us go, then, to Bethlehem to see this thing that has taken place, which the Lord has made known to us." So they went in haste and found Mary and Joseph, and the infant lying in the manger. When they saw this, they made known the message that had been told them about this child. All who heard it were amazed by what had been told them by the shepherds. And Mary kept all these things, reflecting on them in her heart. Then the shepherds returned, glorifying and praising God for all they had heard and seen, just as it had been told to them.

First Reading (Isa 62:11-12)

See, the LORD proclaims
   to the ends of the earth:
say to daughter Zion,
   your savior comes!
Here is his reward with him,
   his recompense before him.
They shall be called the holy people,
   the redeemed of the LORD,
and you shall be called "Frequented,"
   a city that is not forsaken.

Responsorial Psalm (Ps 97:1, 6, 11-12)

℟. A light will shine on us this day: the Lord is born for us.

The LORD is king; let the earth rejoice;
   let the many isles be glad.
The heavens proclaim his justice,
   and all peoples see his glory.

℟. A light will shine on us this day: the Lord is born for us.

Light dawns for the just;
and gladness, for the upright of heart.
Be glad in the LORD, you just,
and give thanks to his holy name.

R⁊. A light will shine on us this day: the Lord is born for us.

See Appendix, p. 201, for Second Reading

Reflecting on Living the Gospel

The shepherds who feature so prominently in today's gospel are name-
less, foreshadowing the scores of disciples, members of the crowds, and
various onlookers that Jesus will attract throughout his short life. Where
do we find ourselves in such a picture? Do we seek Jesus this morning
because of an angelic apparition? Or because someone else told us about
him, much like the shepherds told many others? Or are we the evangeliz-
ers, drawing others to the Savior? This child, Jesus, is destined to be the
rise and fall of many. What will be our role in this drama?

Connecting the Responsorial Psalm to the Readings

The gospel reading for this Mass focuses on the response of the shepherds to the message brought to them by the angel of the Lord. We can
imagine the scene as light bursting forth into darkness as the angel appears and the "glory of the Lord" shines around the frightened men.
Once this light recedes with the angels returning to heaven, the shepherds go in search of the true Light and find him with Mary and Joseph,
"lying in the manger." The responsorial psalm alludes to the light that
shines in the darkness: "A light will shine on us this day: the Lord is born
for us."

Psalmist Preparation

Which places of darkness within your own life would you like to offer to
the Lord of Light this day?

Prayer

With every dawn, as with every birth,
your mercies, O God, are renewed for us.
Let us go in haste to make your message known.
The Lord is born for us this day.
With heaven and earth, let us rejoice. Amen.

DECEMBER 25, 2019

Gospel (John 1:1-18
[or John 1:1-5, 9-14]; L16ABC)

In the beginning was the Word,
and the Word was with God,
and the Word was God.
He was in the beginning with God.
All things came to be through him,
and without him nothing came to be.
What came to be through him was life,
and this life was the light of the
human race;
the light shines in the darkness,
and the darkness has not overcome it.

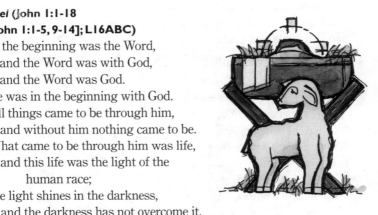

A man named John was sent from God. He came for testimony, to testify to the light, so that all might believe through him. He was not the light, but came to testify to the light. The true light, which enlightens everyone, was coming into the world.

He was in the world,
and the world came to be through him,
but the world did not know him.
He came to what was his own,
but his own people did not accept him.

But to those who did accept him he gave power to become children of God, to those who believe in his name, who were born not by natural generation nor by human choice nor by a man's decision but of God.

And the Word became flesh
and made his dwelling among us,
and we saw his glory,
the glory as of the Father's only Son,
full of grace and truth.

John testified to him and cried out, saying, "This was he of whom I said, 'The one who is coming after me ranks ahead of me because he existed before me.'" From his fullness we have all received, grace in place of grace, because while the law was given through Moses, grace and truth came through Jesus Christ. No one has ever seen God. The only Son, God, who is at the Father's side, has revealed him.

First Reading (Isa 52:7-10)

How beautiful upon the mountains
    are the feet of him who brings glad tidings,
announcing peace, bearing good news,
    announcing salvation, and saying to Zion,
    "Your God is King!"

Hark! Your sentinels raise a cry,
    together they shout for joy,
for they see directly, before their eyes,
    the Lord restoring Zion.
Break out together in song,
    O ruins of Jerusalem!
For the Lord comforts his people,
    he redeems Jerusalem.
The Lord has bared his holy arm
    in the sight of all the nations;
all the ends of the earth will behold
    the salvation of our God.

Responsorial Psalm (Ps 98:1, 2-3, 3-4, 5-6)

R℣. (3c) All the ends of the earth have seen the saving power of God.

Sing to the Lord a new song,
    for he has done wondrous deeds;
his right hand has won victory for him,
    his holy arm.

R℣. All the ends of the earth have seen the saving power of God.

The Lord has made his salvation known:
    in the sight of the nations he has revealed his justice.
He has remembered his kindness and his faithfulness
    toward the house of Israel.

R℣. All the ends of the earth have seen the saving power of God.

All the ends of the earth have seen
    the salvation by our God.
Sing joyfully to the Lord, all you lands;
    break into song; sing praise.

R℣. All the ends of the earth have seen the saving power of God.

Sing praise to the Lord with the harp,
    with the harp and melodious song.
With trumpets and the sound of the horn
    sing joyfully before the King, the Lord.

R℣. All the ends of the earth have seen the saving power of God.

See Appendix, p. 202, for Second Reading

Reflecting on Living the Gospel

It is no coincidence that the opening words of John's prologue proclaimed at Christmas, "In the beginning" (John 1:1), are the same words we hear at the Easter Vigil in the story of creation from Genesis. John's theological hymn begins the evangelist's gradual revelation of Christ's identity, from divine Word spoken from the beginning, to Word made flesh in the life of Jesus, to Word of life breathed from the cross from the Son's spirit commended back to the Father with whom he is one from the beginning.

Connecting the Responsorial Psalm to the Readings

In our psalm for this liturgy, we find the command to "sing" five times. This is the only proper response the psalmist can propose for the wonder and glory wrought by our God and Lord. At Christmas we celebrate especially the second person of the Trinity, God, the Son, born in Bethlehem some two thousand years ago. In the second reading and the gospel, we hear especially about the magnificent nature of this baby, for it is through the Son that God "created the universe," the letter to the Hebrews proclaims, and "without him nothing came to be," John's gospel tells us.

Psalmist Preparation

As a cantor, you lead the people of God in fulfilling the psalmist's command to "sing joyfully" and "sing praise" to the One who has brought salvation to the ends of the earth. How does this joy reverberate in your life of faith?

Prayer

In the beginning was your Word, O God,
giving life to all that lives.
May your Word be the song we sing this day and always.
All the ends of the earth have seen
the saving power of God. Amen.

Gospel (Matt 2:13-15, 19-23; L17A)

When the magi had departed, behold, the angel of the Lord appeared to Joseph in a dream and said, "Rise, take the child and his mother, flee to Egypt, and stay there until I tell you. Herod is going to search for the child to destroy him." Joseph rose and took the child and his mother by night and departed for Egypt. He stayed there until the death of Herod, that what the Lord had said through the prophet might be fulfilled,

Out of Egypt I called my son.

When Herod had died, behold, the angel of the Lord appeared in a dream to Joseph in Egypt and said, "Rise, take the child and his mother and go to the land of Israel, for those who sought the child's life are dead." He rose, took the child and his mother, and went to the land of Israel. But when he heard that Archelaus was ruling over Judea in place of his father Herod, he was afraid to go back there. And because he had been warned in a dream, he departed for the region of Galilee. He went and dwelt in a town called Nazareth, so that what had been spoken through the prophets might be fulfilled,

He shall be called a Nazorean.

First Reading (Sir 3:2-6, 12-14)

God sets a father in honor over his children;
    a mother's authority he confirms over her sons.
Whoever honors his father atones for sins,
    and preserves himself from them.
When he prays, he is heard;
    he stores up riches who reveres his mother.
Whoever honors his father is gladdened by children,
    and, when he prays, is heard.
Whoever reveres his father will live a long life;
    he who obeys his father brings comfort to his mother.

My son, take care of your father when he is old;
    grieve him not as long as he lives.

Even if his mind fail, be considerate of him;
    revile him not all the days of his life;
kindness to a father will not be forgotten,
    firmly planted against the debt of your sins
    —a house raised in justice to you.

Responsorial Psalm (Ps 128:1-2, 3, 4-5)

R̂. (cf. 1) Blessed are those who fear the Lord and walk in his ways.

Blessed is everyone who fears the LORD,
    who walks in his ways!
For you shall eat the fruit of your handiwork;
    blessed shall you be, and favored.

R̂. Blessed are those who fear the Lord and walk in his ways.

Your wife shall be like a fruitful vine
    in the recesses of your home;
your children like olive plants
    around your table.

R̂. Blessed are those who fear the Lord and walk in his ways.

Behold, thus is the man blessed
    who fears the LORD.
The LORD bless you from Zion:
    may you see the prosperity of Jerusalem
    all the days of your life.

R̂. Blessed are those who fear the Lord and walk in his ways.

See Appendix, p. 202, for Second Reading

Reflecting on Living the Gospel

With today's gospel we are reminded that Joseph, Mary, and the child Jesus were political refugees. They feared for their lives, as Herod had massacred the innocents. The Holy Family found safety and refuge in a foreign country. Though Jesus was Emmanuel, danger was present and must have seemed a specter shadowing the Holy Family. We know that Jesus will ultimately lose his life at the hands of the state. Is it any wonder that the gospel message was so popular with the outcast and marginalized? Let us, as disciples, identify with the outcast, marginalized, and afflicted, for that is how the Holy Family lived.

THE HOLY FAMILY OF JESUS, MARY, AND JOSEPH

Connecting the Responsorial Psalm to the Readings

Today's psalm paints an idyllic picture of the family life waiting for those "who fear the Lord and walk in his ways." While we know that there is no guarantee of creating this type of family (spouse and children) based on our faith alone, we also know that we are all a part of the holy family of God. As St. Paul reminds us in his letter to the Colossians, God's holy family is brought together whenever people "put on . . . compassion, kindness, humility, [and] gentleness" in their dealings with one another.

Psalmist Preparation

In your ministry as a cantor, how do you help to create the holy family of God within your parish? When have you been most grateful for this parish family in your life?

Prayer

With a father's love and a mother's care,
you have made us your children, O God.
Make our families holy not by perfection but by love.
May the peace of Christ be in our hearts.
May the word of Christ dwell in us richly. Amen.

Gospel (Luke 2:16-21; L18ABC)

The shepherds went in haste to Bethlehem and
found Mary and Joseph, and the infant lying in
the manger. When they saw this, they made
known the message that had been told them
about this child. All who heard it were amazed
by what had been told them by the shepherds.
And Mary kept all these things, reflecting on
them in her heart. Then the shepherds returned, glorifying and praising God for all
they had heard and seen, just as it had
been told to them.

When eight days were completed for
his circumcision, he was named Jesus, the
name given him by the angel before he was conceived in the womb.

First Reading (Num 6:22-27)

The LORD said to Moses: "Speak to Aaron and his sons and tell them:
This is how you shall bless the Israelites. Say to them:

> The LORD bless you and keep you!
> The LORD let his face shine upon you, and be gracious to you!
> The LORD look upon you kindly and give you peace!

So shall they invoke my name upon the Israelites, and I will bless them."

Responsorial Psalm (Ps 67:2-3, 5, 6, 8)

℟. (2a) May God bless us in his mercy.

May God have pity on us and bless us;
  may he let his face shine upon us.
So may your way be known upon earth;
  among all nations, your salvation.

℟. May God bless us in his mercy.

May the nations be glad and exult
  because you rule the peoples in equity;
  the nations on the earth you guide.

℟. May God bless us in his mercy.

May the peoples praise you, O God;
    may all the peoples praise you!
May God bless us,
    and may all the ends of the earth fear him!

R̸. May God bless us in his mercy.

See Appendix, p. 202, for Second Reading

Reflecting on Living the Gospel
Jesus imbibed the religious values of his parents and lived them out in a dramatic way. He was no divine puppet. Instead, Luke tells us that Jesus "grew and became strong," and he "advanced [in] wisdom and age and favor before God and man" (Luke 2:40, 52; NABRE). We too can allow ourselves and others to grow in wisdom. None of us has all the answers; we rely on others for advice. Let us continue to set aside our own hubris and pride, being open to the influence of others who can help us grow in wisdom and knowledge.

Connecting the Responsorial Psalm to the Readings
Within both the responsorial psalm and the first reading, we find the phrase, may the Lord "let his face shine upon you (us)." As we complete the octave of Christmas, we continue to meditate on the birth of "the light [that] shines in the darkness" that "the darkness has not overcome" (John 1:5; NABRE). Just as Mary nurtures and protects the infant in the manger, she also nurtures this light within her own heart, contemplating it in holy silence.

Psalmist Preparation
As we enter into the new calendar year, let us attune our own lives and hearts to the light of God's face shining upon us. Where does this light burn most brightly in your life?

Prayer
At the dawn of this New Year of grace, O Lord,
help us be present each day, like Mary,
to the blessings you have prepared for your people.
May God bless us in his mercy;
may the nations be glad and exult. Amen.

Gospel (Matt 2:1-12; L20ABC)

When Jesus was born in Bethlehem of Judea, in the days of King Herod, behold, magi from the east arrived in Jerusalem, saying, "Where is the newborn king of the Jews? We saw his star at its rising and have come to do him homage." When King Herod heard this, he was greatly troubled, and all Jerusalem with him. Assembling all the chief priests and the scribes of the people, he inquired of them where the Christ was to be born. They said to him, "In Bethlehem of Judea, for thus it has been written through the prophet:

> *And you, Bethlehem, land of Judah,*
> *are by no means least among the rulers of Judah;*
> *since from you shall come a ruler,*
> *who is to shepherd my people Israel."*

Then Herod called the magi secretly and ascertained from them the time of the star's appearance. He sent them to Bethlehem and said, "Go and search diligently for the child. When you have found him, bring me word, that I too may go and do him homage." After their audience with the king they set out. And behold, the star that they had seen at its rising preceded them, until it came and stopped over the place where the child was. They were overjoyed at seeing the star, and on entering the house they saw the child with Mary his mother. They prostrated themselves and did him homage. Then they opened their treasures and offered him gifts of gold, frankincense, and myrrh. And having been warned in a dream not to return to Herod, they departed for their country by another way.

First Reading (Isa 60:1-6)

> Rise up in splendor, Jerusalem! Your light has come,
> the glory of the Lord shines upon you.
> See, darkness covers the earth,
> and thick clouds cover the peoples;
> but upon you the Lord shines,
> and over you appears his glory.
> Nations shall walk by your light,
> and kings by your shining radiance.

Raise your eyes and look about;
  they all gather and come to you:
your sons come from afar,
  and your daughters in the arms of their nurses.

Then you shall be radiant at what you see,
  your heart shall throb and overflow,
for the riches of the sea shall be emptied out before you,
  the wealth of nations shall be brought to you.
Caravans of camels shall fill you,
  dromedaries from Midian and Ephah;
all from Sheba shall come
  bearing gold and frankincense,
  and proclaiming the praises of the LORD.

Responsorial Psalm (Ps 72:1-2, 7-8, 10-11, 12-13)

R℣. (cf. 11) Lord, every nation on earth will adore you.

O God, with your judgment endow the king,
  and with your justice, the king's son;
he shall govern your people with justice
  and your afflicted ones with judgment.

R℣. Lord, every nation on earth will adore you.

Justice shall flower in his days,
  and profound peace, till the moon be no more.
May he rule from sea to sea,
  and from the River to the ends of the earth.

R℣. Lord, every nation on earth will adore you.

The kings of Tarshish and the Isles shall offer gifts;
  the kings of Arabia and Seba shall bring tribute.
All kings shall pay him homage,
  all nations shall serve him.

R℣. Lord, every nation on earth will adore you.

For he shall rescue the poor when he cries out,
  and the afflicted when he has no one to help him.
He shall have pity for the lowly and the poor;
  the lives of the poor he shall save.

R℣. Lord, every nation on earth will adore you.

See Appendix, p. 203, for Second Reading

Reflecting on Living the Gospel

The magi in today's gospel represent all those who are not part of the "in" crowd. These foreigners come to worship Jesus before anyone else does. They recognize in the signs of nature that something significant has happened, and they seek it out. Those who should know their own Scriptures missed something that Zoroastrian priests perceived. We ask ourselves, too, what we might miss when signs are right in front of our eyes. What is God doing in our midst? Is it something that others—foreigners, those not part of the "in" crowd—notice, but it escapes our attention? May we have eyes to see and ears to hear.

Connecting the Responsorial Psalm to the Readings

Today's psalm offers a vision of kings traveling from far-off lands to pay tribute to the king of Israel who will bring about justice and peace in his time. When we consider a king, we might think of a palace, riches, servants, and luxury. This is not what the magi found when they traveled from afar to seek the "newborn king of the Jews." Instead, the child and his mother dwell in a simple house in Bethlehem. And yet, the magi offer gifts and prostrate themselves in worship.

Psalmist Preparation

God, the King, comes to us in the ordinary form of a toddler in the small town of Bethlehem. The word "epiphany" means manifestation or revelation. Where do you find God manifested or revealed in your life?

Prayer

Where darkness covers the earth, your glory, Lord, shines.
Where nations walk in fear, your star lights the way.
Help us always to follow where you lead.
All you lands, raise your eyes and see:
Our God has come to save us. Amen.

Gospel (Matt 3:13-17; L21A)

Jesus came from Galilee to John at the Jordan to be baptized by him. John tried to prevent him, saying, "I need to be baptized by you, and yet you are coming to me?" Jesus said to him in reply, "Allow it now, for thus it is fitting for us to fulfill all righteousness." Then he allowed him. After Jesus was baptized, he came up from the water and behold, the heavens were opened for him, and he saw the Spirit of God descending like a dove and coming upon him. And a voice came from the heavens, saying, "This is my beloved Son, with whom I am well pleased."

First Reading (Isa 42:1-4, 6-7)

Thus says the LORD:

Here is my servant whom I uphold,
my chosen one with whom I am pleased,
upon whom I have put my spirit;
he shall bring forth justice to the nations,
not crying out, not shouting,
not making his voice heard in the street.
A bruised reed he shall not break,
and a smoldering wick he shall not quench,
until he establishes justice on the earth;
the coastlands will wait for his teaching.

I, the LORD, have called you for the victory of justice,
I have grasped you by the hand;
I formed you, and set you
as a covenant of the people,
a light for the nations,
to open the eyes of the blind,
to bring out prisoners from confinement,
and from the dungeon, those who live in darkness.

Responsorial Psalm (Ps 29:1-2, 3-4, 9-10)

℟. (11b) The Lord will bless his people with peace.

Give to the LORD, you sons of God,
   give to the LORD glory and praise,
give to the LORD the glory due his name;
   adore the LORD in holy attire.

℟. The Lord will bless his people with peace.

The voice of the LORD is over the waters,
   the LORD, over vast waters.
The voice of the LORD is mighty;
   the voice of the LORD is majestic.

℟. The Lord will bless his people with peace.

The God of glory thunders,
   and in his temple all say, "Glory!"
The LORD is enthroned above the flood;
   the LORD is enthroned as king forever.

℟. The Lord will bless his people with peace.

See Appendix, p. 203, for Second Reading

Reflecting on Living the Gospel

Baptism is an ancient practice with some roots in the Essene community and in the ministry of John. Many of those ancient Jewish people who felt a need to repent of sin and experience forgiveness were baptized by John in the Jordan. How strange then that Jesus, too, went to John to be baptized. Each evangelist handles the matter in a slightly different way, with the Gospel of John skipping the baptism altogether, so that John simply testifies to Jesus as the Lamb of God! On this feast of the baptism, let us recall the meaning of our own baptism and live lives worthy of that call.

Connecting the Responsorial Psalm to the Readings

In the responsorial psalm, the image of water is evoked twice. We hear that "the voice of the Lord is over the waters, / the Lord, over vast waters." And then that "[t]he Lord is enthroned above the flood." The first image reminds us of the waters of creation when "a mighty wind" swept over the waters (Gen 1:2; NABRE), the second of the great flood that washes creation clean again in the time of Noah. Both of these moments are referred to in the Rite of Baptism when the water in the font is blessed. The presider prays, "At the very dawn of creation your Spirit breathed on the waters, making them the wellspring of holiness. The waters of the great flood you made a sign of the waters of baptism, that make an end of sin and a new beginning of goodness" (54).

Psalmist Preparation

In our everyday life, water cleanses and sustains us. How do you celebrate, remember, and renew the cleansing, sustain power of your own baptism?

Prayer

Upon your Son, your favor rests, O God,
and through his baptism, you opened heaven to all who believe.
In Christ, may we be ever pleasing in your sight.
Give to the Lord glory and praise!
Glory to God in the highest! Amen.

JANUARY 19, 2020

Gospel (John 1:29-34; L64A)

John the Baptist saw Jesus coming toward him and said, "Behold, the Lamb of God, who takes away the sin of the world. He is the one of whom I said, 'A man is coming after me who ranks ahead of me because he existed before me.' I did not know him, but the reason why I came baptizing with water was that he might be made known to Israel." John testified further, saying, "I saw the Spirit come down like a dove from heaven and remain upon him. I did not know him, but the one who sent me to baptize with water told me, 'On whomever you see the Spirit come down and remain, he is the one who will baptize with the Holy Spirit.' Now I have seen and testified that he is the Son of God."

First Reading (Isa 49:3, 5-6)

The LORD said to me: You are my servant,
    Israel, through whom I show my glory.
Now the LORD has spoken
    who formed me as his servant from the womb,
that Jacob may be brought back to him
    and Israel gathered to him;
and I am made glorious in the sight of the LORD,
    and my God is now my strength!
It is too little, the LORD says, for you to be my servant,
    to raise up the tribes of Jacob,
    and restore the survivors of Israel;
I will make you a light to the nations,
    that my salvation may reach to the ends of the earth.

Responsorial Psalm (Ps 40:2, 4, 7-8, 8-9, 10)

℞. (8a and 9a) Here am I, Lord; I come to do your will.

I have waited, waited for the LORD,
    and he stooped toward me and heard my cry.
And he put a new song into my mouth,
    a hymn to our God.

℞. Here am I, Lord; I come to do your will.

Sacrifice or offering you wished not,
  but ears open to obedience you gave me.
Holocausts or sin-offerings you sought not;
  then said I, "Behold I come."

R̶⁊. Here am I, Lord; I come to do your will.

"In the written scroll it is prescribed for me,
to do your will, O my God, is my delight,
  and your law is within my heart!"

R̶⁊. Here am I, Lord; I come to do your will.

I announced your justice in the vast assembly;
  I did not restrain my lips, as you, O LORD, know.

R̶⁊. Here am I, Lord; I come to do your will.

Second Reading (1 Cor 1:1-3)

Reflecting on Living the Gospel

John the Baptist appears in the Fourth Gospel not to baptize Jesus, but to testify to him. Baptism, this foundational sacrament of water, has a multiplicity of meanings and interpretations in the New Testament and also for us today. When we dip our fingers into the holy water at church, we are reminded that we have been baptized into Christ's death, with the forgiveness of sins. Then we, as his followers, are to testify to him in the world. Our belief in Jesus as the Son of God gives life in his name.

Connecting the Responsorial Psalm to the Readings

Throughout the history of salvation, God has called upon human collaborators to work with him in building the kingdom of God on the earth. In today's responsorial psalm, "Here am I, Lord; I come to do your will," we find the response we can imagine must please the Lord above all others, a ready and willing partner to be God's hands, heart, and love in the world. In the first reading the people of Israel are invited to take on this role, to be the servant through whom God shows his glory, and a light that will reach out to all nations. In the gospel, John the Baptist is the one who heralds the Son of God's presence, and in the second reading St. Paul tells the Corinthians that now it is they who have been sanctified and are "called to be holy."

Psalmist Preparation

God's work, and ours, has not yet been completed. We are the ones who are now invited to tell the Lord, "Here I am, I come to do your will."

Prayer

Your Word, Lord, became flesh and dwelt among us
so that through his Spirit we may become your children.
May we always testify to his saving power.
You have put a new song in our mouths,
a hymn of praise to our gracious God. Amen.

Gospel (Matt 4:12-23 [or Matt 4:12-17]; L67A)

When Jesus heard that John had been arrested, he withdrew to Galilee. He left Nazareth and went to live in Capernaum by the sea, in the region of Zebulun and Naphtali, that what had been said through Isaiah the prophet might be fulfilled:

Land of Zebulun and land
of Naphtali,
the way to the sea, beyond the Jordan,
Galilee of the Gentiles,
the people who sit in darkness have seen a great light,
on those dwelling in a land overshadowed by death
light has arisen.

From that time on, Jesus began to preach and say, "Repent, for the kingdom of heaven is at hand."

As he was walking by the Sea of Galilee, he saw two brothers, Simon who is called Peter, and his brother Andrew, casting a net into the sea; they were fishermen. He said to them, "Come after me, and I will make you fishers of men." At once they left their nets and followed him. He walked along from there and saw two other brothers, James, the son of Zebedee, and his brother John. They were in a boat, with their father Zebedee, mending their nets. He called them, and immediately they left their boat and their father and followed him. He went around all of Galilee, teaching in their synagogues, proclaiming the gospel of the kingdom, and curing every disease and illness among the people.

First Reading (Isa 8:23–9:3)

First the Lord degraded the land of Zebulun and the land of Naphtali; but in the end he has glorified the seaward road, the land west of the Jordan, the District of the Gentiles.

Anguish has taken wing, dispelled is darkness:
for there is no gloom where but now there was distress.
The people who walked in darkness
have seen a great light;

upon those who dwelt in the land of gloom
　　a light has shone.
You have brought them abundant joy
　　and great rejoicing,
as they rejoice before you as at the harvest,
　　as people make merry when dividing spoils.
For the yoke that burdened them,
　　the pole on their shoulder,
and the rod of their taskmaster
　　you have smashed, as on the day of Midian.

Responsorial Psalm (Ps 27:1, 4, 13-14)

℟. (1a) The Lord is my light and my salvation.

The LORD is my light and my salvation;
　　whom should I fear?
The LORD is my life's refuge;
　　of whom should I be afraid?

℟. The Lord is my light and my salvation.

One thing I ask of the LORD;
　　this I seek:
to dwell in the house of the LORD
　　all the days of my life,
that I may gaze on the loveliness of the LORD
　　and contemplate his temple.

℟. The Lord is my light and my salvation.

I believe that I shall see the bounty of the LORD
　　in the land of the living.
Wait for the LORD with courage;
　　be stouthearted, and wait for the LORD.

℟. The Lord is my light and my salvation.

Second Reading (1 Cor 1:10-13, 17)

Reflecting on Living the Gospel

Jesus called the disciples near the beginning of his ministry. And he called them two by two, the brothers Simon and Andrew, and James and John. These were fishermen, in some ways the ancient equivalent of today's highly skilled blue-collar workers. They worked with their hands, as even the "mending their nets" indicates. At the invitation of Jesus, they all leave behind their way of life to follow him. Modern calls to discipleship are scarcely so dramatic. Even so, we are called to put aside the tedious, monotonous, quotidian activities that mark our lives and enter into a new relationship with Christ.

Connecting the Responsorial Psalm to the Readings

Imagery of light echoes throughout the first reading, the gospel, and the responsorial psalm. We sing together, "The Lord is my light and my salvation." What does this mean? How is Jesus like a light for us? Isaiah gives us a clue when he prophesies, "The people who walked in darkness / have seen a great light." There is an immense difference between trying to walk in darkness and walking in light. In darkness we are unaware of where our steps are taking us or what dangers and obstacles might be in our path. In the gospel these words of the prophet are changed slightly to tell us, "[T]he people who sit in darkness have seen a great light / on those dwelling in a land overshadowed by death / light has arisen." To *sit* in darkness conjures an image of hopelessness and despair. We are consumed by the darkness that covers us and see no way of escape. Within this state it is easy to see how one might become "overshadowed by death," a term that could mean despair or loss of hope and joy.

Psalmist Preparation

How do you experience Jesus as "light" and "salvation"?

Prayer

Your Son, O God, fulfilled your promise
to bring light to all overshadowed by death.
May we dwell with Christ in your house all our days.
The Lord is my light and my salvation;
No one shall I fear. Amen.

Gospel (Luke 2:22-40 [or shorter form below 2:22-32]; L524)

When the days were completed for their purification
    according to the law of Moses,
    Mary and Joseph took Jesus up to
        Jerusalem
    to present him to the Lord,
    just as it is written in the law of
        the Lord,
    Every male that opens the womb
        shall be consecrated to
        the Lord,
    and to offer the sacrifice of
    a pair of turtledoves or two young
        pigeons,
    in accordance with the dictate in the law of the Lord.

Now there was a man in Jerusalem whose name was Simeon.
This man was righteous and devout,
    awaiting the consolation of Israel,
    and the Holy Spirit was upon him.
It had been revealed to him by the Holy Spirit
    that he should not see death
    before he had seen the Christ of the Lord.
He came in the Spirit into the temple;
    and when the parents brought in the child Jesus
    to perform the custom of the law in regard to him,
    he took him into his arms and blessed God, saying:
        "Now, Master, you may let your servant go
            in peace, according to your word,
        for my eyes have seen your salvation,
            which you prepared in sight of all the peoples,
        a light for revelation to the Gentiles,
            and glory for your people Israel."

First Reading (Mal 3:1-4)

    Thus says the Lord GOD:
Lo, I am sending my messenger
    to prepare the way before me;
and suddenly there will come to the temple
    the LORD whom you seek,

and the messenger of the covenant whom you desire.
    Yes, he is coming, says the LORD of hosts.
But who will endure the day of his coming?
    And who can stand when he appears?
For he is like the refiner's fire,
    or like the fuller's lye.
He will sit refining and purifying silver,
    and he will purify the sons of Levi,
refining them like gold or like silver
    that they may offer due sacrifice to the LORD.
Then the sacrifice of Judah and Jerusalem
    will please the LORD,
    as in the days of old, as in years gone by.

Responsorial Psalm (Ps 24:7, 8, 9, 10)

R℣. (8) Who is this king of glory? It is the Lord!

Lift up, O gates, your lintels;
    reach up, you ancient portals,
    that the king of glory may come in!

R℣. Who is this king of glory? It is the Lord!

Who is this king of glory?
    The LORD, strong and mighty,
    the LORD, mighty in battle.

R℣. Who is this king of glory? It is the Lord!

Lift up, O gates, your lintels;
    reach up, you ancient portals,
    that the king of glory may come in!

R℣. Who is this king of glory? It is the Lord!

Who is this king of glory?
    The LORD of hosts; he is the king of glory.

R℣. Who is this king of glory? It is the Lord!

Second Reading (Heb 2:14-18)

Reflecting on Living the Gospel

It should go without saying that women figure prominently in some of
the most remembered stories about Jesus, including his birth, death, and
resurrection. And today we have the story of his presentation, accompa-

nied by the presence of Simeon and Anna, as women speak the powerful words of God just as men do. When given the opportunity, let us showcase this too often neglected aspect of our rich faith. And in our own world, in our own day and age, let's listen attentively to the prophetesses in our own midst. Luke gives equal voice to the women. We would do well to follow his example.

Connecting the Responsorial Psalm to the Readings

The readings today invite us to hold in tension multiple images of our Lord and Savior. The prophet Malachi paints a picture of the one who is coming as "refiner's fire," sent to purify the people. In the letter to the Hebrews, Jesus is the high priest who "expiate[s] the sins of the people" through his own body and blood. In the gospel, he is a helpless baby only a little over a month old, and in today's psalm he is the king of glory, a mighty warrior.

Psalmist Preparation

Within our faith we can look at each of these images and we say, "[Y]es, this is our Lord," and yet, often as individual Christians we will find a particular way of looking at Jesus that resonates most within us. No single image, metaphor, or simile can encompass all aspects of Jesus, the Son of God, the second person of the Holy Trinity. Within today's readings, is there a way of considering Jesus that is new for you? How might this image deepen your relationship with Christ?

Prayer

Our eyes have seen your salvation, Lord,
in the promise of a child given to us: Jesus, the King of glory.
Help us to recognize him in our midst.
Send us in peace, O God,
to announce what we have seen. Amen.

Gospel (Matt 5:13-16; L73A)

Jesus said to his disciples: "You are the salt of the earth. But if salt loses its taste, with what can it be seasoned? It is no longer good for anything but to be thrown out and trampled underfoot. You are the light of the world. A city set on a mountain cannot be hidden. Nor do they light a lamp and then put it under a bushel basket; it is set on a lampstand, where it gives light to all in the house. Just so, your light must shine before others, that they may see your good deeds and glorify your heavenly Father."

First Reading (Isa 58:7-10)

Thus says the LORD:
Share your bread with the hungry,
shelter the oppressed and the homeless;
clothe the naked when you see them,
and do not turn your back on your own.
Then your light shall break forth like the dawn,
and your wound shall quickly be healed;
your vindication shall go before you,
and the glory of the LORD shall be your rear guard.
Then you shall call, and the LORD will answer,
you shall cry for help, and he will say: Here I am!
If you remove from your midst
oppression, false accusation and malicious speech;
if you bestow your bread on the hungry
and satisfy the afflicted;
then light shall rise for you in the darkness,
and the gloom shall become for you like midday.

Responsorial Psalm (Ps 112:4-5, 6-7, 8-9)

℟. (4a) The just man is a light in darkness to the upright. *or:* ℟. Alleluia.

Light shines through the darkness for the upright;
    he is gracious and merciful and just.
Well for the man who is gracious and lends,
    who conducts his affairs with justice.

℟. The just man is a light in darkness to the upright. *or:* ℟. Alleluia.

He shall never be moved;
    the just one shall be in everlasting remembrance.
An evil report he shall not fear;
    his heart is firm, trusting in the LORD.

℟. The just man is a light in darkness to the upright. *or:* ℟. Alleluia.

His heart is steadfast; he shall not fear.
    Lavishly he gives to the poor;
his justice shall endure forever;
    his horn shall be exalted in glory.

℟. The just man is a light in darkness to the upright. *or:* ℟. Alleluia.

Second Reading (1 Cor 2:1-5)

Reflecting on Living the Gospel
The gospel opens with the words "Jesus said to his disciples," thus giving us not only an account of something two thousand years ago, but something that is addressed to us today. There are two "you are" statements that cannot be missed. The metaphors are simple but sublime: "salt" and "light." Jesus is telling his disciples as he tells us that we are the salt for the earth and the light of the world. What an impressive moniker! Are we up to it? Whether or not we deem the terms appropriate appellations, we are given those names nonetheless.

Connecting the Responsorial Psalm to the Readings
To the imagery of light found in both the first reading and the gospel, the psalmist also highlights the firm foundation of the just. We are told that the upright one "shall never be moved" and that his heart is "firm" and "steadfast." In the gospel reading Jesus likens his disciples to a city on a hill that "cannot be hidden." The psalmist's characterization of the just one leads to another image; like a lighthouse "the just man is a light in darkness."

Psalmist Preparation

Who has been an example of faith and a guiding light for you in times of darkness? How are you being called to be this light for others?

Prayer

Jesus is the light of the world.
In him let our light shine before others
that all may glorify you, heavenly Father.
The light of Christ shines through the darkness;
a light for all to see. Amen.

FEBRUARY 16, 2020

Gospel (Matt 5:17-37 [or shorter form below Matt 5:20-22a, 27-28, 33-34a, 37]; L76A)

Jesus said to his disciples: "I tell you, unless your righteousness sur-passes that of the scribes and Pharisees, you will not enter the kingdom of heaven.

"You have heard that it was said to your ancestors,

> *You shall not kill; and whoever kills will be liable to judgment.*

But I say to you, whoever is angry with his brother will be liable to judgment.

"You have heard that it was said, *You shall not commit adultery.* But I say to you, everyone who looks at a woman with lust has already com-mitted adultery with her in his heart.

"Again you have heard that it was said to your ancestors,

> *Do not take a false oath,*
> *but make good to the Lord all that you vow.*

But I say to you, do not swear at all. Let your 'Yes' mean 'Yes,' and your 'No' mean 'No.' Anything more is from the evil one."

First Reading (Sir 15:15-20)

If you choose you can keep the commandments, they will save you;
> if you trust in God, you too shall live;
he has set before you fire and water;
> to whichever you choose, stretch forth your hand.
Before man are life and death, good and evil,
> whichever he chooses shall be given him.
Immense is the wisdom of the Lord;
> he is mighty in power, and all-seeing.
The eyes of God are on those who fear him;
> he understands man's every deed.
No one does he command to act unjustly,
> to none does he give license to sin.

Responsorial Psalm (Ps 119:1-2, 4-5, 17-18, 33-34)

R̸. (1b) Blessed are they who follow the law of the Lord!

Blessed are they whose way is blameless,
 who walk in the law of the LORD.
Blessed are they who observe his decrees,
 who seek him with all their heart.

R̸. Blessed are they who follow the law of the Lord!

You have commanded that your precepts
 be diligently kept.
Oh, that I might be firm in the ways
 of keeping your statutes!

R̸. Blessed are they who follow the law of the Lord!

Be good to your servant, that I may live
 and keep your words.
Open my eyes, that I may consider
 the wonders of your law.

R̸. Blessed are they who follow the law of the Lord!

Instruct me, O LORD, in the way of your statutes,
 that I may exactly observe them.
Give me discernment, that I may observe your law
 and keep it with all my heart.

R̸. Blessed are they who follow the law of the Lord!

Second Reading (1 Cor 2:6-10)

Reflecting on Living the Gospel

To those who want to be right with God but wonder what is the
minimum required to achieve that relationship, Jesus has an answer. We
need to go above and beyond; merely fulfilling the minimum is not
enough. When Jesus responds in this way, we may crave a return to the
minimum! The standard Jesus sets may seem impossible to realize.
When we desire a relationship with Christ for its own sake, and not simply because we've been somehow coerced, a life of faith flows naturally.
We no longer count the minimum but instead live in a relationship of
trust, fidelity, and love.

Connecting the Responsorial Psalm to the Readings

The psalmist proclaims, "Blessed are they who observe his decrees, / who seek him with all their heart." This whole-hearted living is what Jesus calls us to in the gospel and what the author of Sirach describes in the first reading. To live a "blessed" life can sometimes be interpreted as enjoying the gifts of friends, family, and material goods present in one's life. But in this psalm we are told that blessing comes from following God's laws. It is not that we are recompensed with external rewards when we live this way, but that living this way is its own reward.

Psalmist Preparation

Created in the image of God, true peace, fulfillment, and purpose can only be found by delving deeply into the mystery of his love and grace, or as the psalmist says, "the wonders of your law." In your own walk of faith, how do you seek to keep the decrees of God with your whole heart?

Prayer

Blessed are you, Father,
for you have revealed to little ones the mysteries of heaven.
Make our words true and our lives blameless in your sight.
Open our eyes that we may know
the wonders of your law, O God. Amen.

Gospel (Matt 5:38-48; L79A)

Jesus said to his disciples: "You have heard that it was said,

> *An eye for an eye and a tooth for a tooth.*

But I say to you, offer no resistance to one who is evil. When someone strikes you on your right cheek, turn the other one as well. If anyone wants to go to law with you over your tunic, hand over your cloak as well. Should anyone press you into service for one mile, go for two miles. Give to the one who asks of you, and do not turn your back on one who wants to borrow.

"You have heard that it was said,

> *You shall love your neighbor and hate your enemy.*

But I say to you, love your enemies and pray for those who persecute you, that you may be children of your heavenly Father, for he makes his sun rise on the bad and the good, and causes rain to fall on the just and the unjust. For if you love those who love you, what recompense will you have? Do not the tax collectors do the same? And if you greet your brothers only, what is unusual about that? Do not the pagans do the same? So be perfect, just as your heavenly Father is perfect."

First Reading (Lev 19:1-2, 17-18)

The LORD said to Moses, "Speak to the whole Israelite community and tell them: Be holy, for I, the LORD, your God, am holy.

"You shall not bear hatred for your brother or sister in your heart. Though you may have to reprove your fellow citizen, do not incur sin because of him. Take no revenge and cherish no grudge against any of your people. You shall love your neighbor as yourself. I am the LORD."

Responsorial Psalm (Ps 103:1-2, 3-4, 8, 10, 12-13)

℟. (8a) The Lord is kind and merciful.

Bless the LORD, O my soul;
　and all my being, bless his holy name.
Bless the LORD, O my soul,
　and forget not all his benefits.

℟. The Lord is kind and merciful.

He pardons all your iniquities,
　heals all your ills.
He redeems your life from destruction,
　crowns you with kindness and compassion.

℟. The Lord is kind and merciful.

Merciful and gracious is the LORD,
　slow to anger and abounding in kindness.
Not according to our sins does he deal with us,
　nor does he requite us according to our crimes.

℟. The Lord is kind and merciful.

As far as the east is from the west,
　so far has he put our transgressions from us.
As a father has compassion on his children,
　so the LORD has compassion on those who fear him.

℟. The Lord is kind and merciful.

Second Reading (1 Cor 3:16-23)

Reflecting on Living the Gospel

Jesus tells us to pray for one's persecutors rather than to hate them. All too often feelings of exclusion and division can rise up in the face of persecution, which is certainly understandable. Striking back in the face of persecution is a natural human response. Few people have lived up to the ideal that Jesus espouses. If we treat with kindness only those who treat us with kindness, we are merely living the values of the world. Jesus demands that we are "perfect," meaning pure in our devotion to God. Then we will be known as his disciples.

Connecting the Responsorial Psalm to the Readings

The gospel offers us a seemingly impossible commandment: "[B]e perfect, just as your Heavenly Father is perfect." And it *is* impossible to fulfill on our own. As humans, we are not capable of perfection. Only through the merciful kindness of our Creator and Lord are we able to live into these words of Jesus. The psalmist reminds us that in God there is no need for fear. The one who made us "pardons all [our] iniquities, / heals all [our] ills." When we falter and fail, when we sin and wander, our God, in his perfect compassion, redeems us. Removing our transgressions and "crowning us with kindness."

Psalmist Preparation

In striving to be like our heavenly Father, we are called to emulate God's kindness and mercy, to others and to ourselves. Is there a situation in your life that is calling out for mercy and compassion? How might you embrace the perfect love of God as you move forward?

Prayer

Love of neighbor is not enough, O God,
for those who live by your merciful law.
In Christ, help us to love even those we cannot.
Bless the Lord, O my soul;
with all my being, bless God's holy name. Amen.

Gospel (Matt 6:1-6, 16-18; L219)

Jesus said to his disciples: "Take care not to perform righteous deeds in order that people may see them; otherwise, you will have no recompense from your heavenly Father. When you give alms, do not blow a trumpet before you, as the hypocrites do in the synagogues and in the streets to win the praise of others. Amen, I say to you, they have received their reward. But when you give alms, do not let your left hand know what your right is doing, so that your almsgiving may be secret. And your Father who sees in secret will repay you.

"When you pray, do not be like the hypocrites, who love to stand and pray in the synagogues and on street corners so that others may see them. Amen, I say to you, they have received their reward. But when you pray, go to your inner room, close the door, and pray to your Father in secret. And your Father who sees in secret will repay you.

"When you fast, do not look gloomy like the hypocrites. They neglect their appearance, so that they may appear to others to be fasting. Amen, I say to you, they have received their reward. But when you fast, anoint your head and wash your face, so that you may not appear to be fasting, except to your Father who is hidden. And your Father who sees what is hidden will repay you."

First Reading (Joel 2:12-18)

Even now, says the LORD,
    return to me with your whole heart,
    with fasting, and weeping, and mourning;
Rend your hearts, not your garments,
    and return to the LORD, your God.
For gracious and merciful is he,
    slow to anger, rich in kindness,
    and relenting in punishment.
Perhaps he will again relent
    and leave behind him a blessing,
Offerings and libations
    for the LORD, your God.

Blow the trumpet in Zion!
    proclaim a fast,
    call an assembly;
Gather the people,
    notify the congregation;
Assemble the elders,
    gather the children
    and the infants at the breast;
Let the bridegroom quit his room
    and the bride her chamber.
Between the porch and the altar
    let the priests, the ministers of the LORD, weep,
And say, "Spare, O LORD, your people,
    and make not your heritage a reproach,
    with the nations ruling over them!
Why should they say among the peoples,
    'Where is their God?'"

Then the LORD was stirred to concern for his land and took pity on his people.

Responsorial Psalm (Ps 51:3-4, 5-6ab, 12-13, 14, and 17)

R℣. (see 3a) Be merciful, O Lord, for we have sinned.

Have mercy on me, O God, in your goodness;
    in the greatness of your compassion wipe out my offense.
Thoroughly wash me from my guilt
    and of my sin cleanse me.

R℣. Be merciful, O Lord, for we have sinned.

For I acknowledge my offense,
    and my sin is before me always:
"Against you only have I sinned,
    and done what is evil in your sight."

R℣. Be merciful, O Lord, for we have sinned.

A clean heart create for me, O God,
    and a steadfast spirit renew within me.
Cast me not out from your presence,
    and your Holy Spirit take not from me.

R℣. Be merciful, O Lord, for we have sinned.

Give me back the joy of your salvation,
   and a willing spirit sustain in me.
O Lord, open my lips,
   and my mouth shall proclaim your praise.

℞. Be merciful, O Lord, for we have sinned.

See Appendix, p. 203, for Second Reading

Reflecting on Living the Gospel

As we initiate our Lenten season with Ash Wednesday, we are dramatically reminded that our lives will come to an end. What remains of us on this earth are only ashes. By wearing this stark sacramental marking us as Christians today, we know that this life is but a prelude to another. Any quest for fortune and fame ought to be tempered with our call to give alms, fast, and pray. As disciples, we have only one audience, which is God in heaven. Let us act mercifully toward one another for the sake of God, giving alms, fasting, and praying in a quiet, humble way.

Connecting the Responsorial Psalm to the Readings

Today the psalmist cries out, "A clean heart create for me, O God, / and a steadfast spirit renew within me." In this prayer, we find the core of Lenten spirituality. We take on the practices of prayer, fasting, and almsgiving that Jesus commends to us in the gospel, not for the sake of repentance alone, but so that we might be made new in the process.

Psalmist Preparation

Along with the catechumens, the entire church is on a journey to the baptismal font, the wellspring of new life. This Lent, where are you in need of renewal and cleansing?

Prayer

In this acceptable time, on this day of salvation,
create in us new hearts, O God, that we may hear your Son's voice
and turn our lives to follow your Gospel.
Blow the trumpet, and proclaim a fast,
for God is here with grace for his people. Amen.

Gospel (Matt 4:1-11; L22A)

At that time Jesus was led by the Spirit into the desert to be tempted by the devil. He fasted for forty days and forty nights, and afterwards he was hungry. The tempter approached and said to him, "If you are the Son of God, command that these stones become loaves of bread." He said in reply, "It is written:

One does not live on bread alone,
but on every word that comes forth
from the mouth of God."

Then the devil took him to the holy city, and made him stand on the parapet of the temple, and said to him, "If you are the Son of God, throw yourself down. For it is written:

He will command his angels concerning you
and with their hands they will support you,
lest you dash your foot against a stone."

Jesus answered him, "Again it is written,

You shall not put the Lord, your God, to the test."

Then the devil took him up to a very high mountain, and showed him all the kingdoms of the world in their magnificence, and he said to him, "All these I shall give to you, if you will prostrate yourself and worship me." At this, Jesus said to him, "Get away, Satan! It is written:

The Lord, your God, shall you worship
and him alone shall you serve."

Then the devil left him and, behold, angels came and ministered to him.

First Reading (Gen 2:7-9; 3:1-7)

The LORD God formed man out of the clay of the ground and blew into his nostrils the breath of life, and so man became a living being.

Then the LORD God planted a garden in Eden, in the east, and placed there the man whom he had formed. Out of the ground the LORD God made various trees grow that were delightful to look at and good for food, with the tree of life in the middle of the garden and the tree of the knowledge of good and evil.

Now the serpent was the most cunning of all the animals that the LORD God had made. The serpent asked the woman, "Did God really tell you not to eat from any of the trees in the garden?" The woman answered the serpent: "We may eat of the fruit of the trees in the garden; it is only about the fruit of the tree in the middle of the garden that God said, 'You shall not eat it or even touch it, lest you die.'" But the serpent said to the woman: "You certainly will not die! No, God knows well that the moment you eat of it your eyes will be opened and you will be like gods who know what is good and what is evil." The woman saw that the tree was good for food, pleasing to the eyes, and desirable for gaining wisdom. So she took some of its fruit and ate it; and she also gave some to her husband, who was with her, and he ate it. Then the eyes of both of them were opened, and they realized that they were naked; so they sewed fig leaves together and made loincloths for themselves.

Responsorial Psalm (Ps 51:3-4, 5-6, 12-13, 17)

R⁊. (cf. 3a) Be merciful, O Lord, for we have sinned.

Have mercy on me, O God, in your goodness;
    in the greatness of your compassion wipe out my offense.
Thoroughly wash me from my guilt
    and of my sin cleanse me.

R⁊. Be merciful, O Lord, for we have sinned.

For I acknowledge my offense,
    and my sin is before me always:
"Against you only have I sinned,
    and done what is evil in your sight."

R⁊. Be merciful, O Lord, for we have sinned.

A clean heart create for me, O God,
    and a steadfast spirit renew within me.
Cast me not out from your presence,
    and your Holy Spirit take not from me.

R⁊. Be merciful, O Lord, for we have sinned.

Give me back the joy of your salvation,
    and a willing spirit sustain in me.
O Lord, open my lips,
    and my mouth shall proclaim your praise.

R⁊. Be merciful, O Lord, for we have sinned.

See Appendix, p. 203, for Second Reading

Reflecting on Living the Gospel

Today's gospel invites us to consider the human condition from the viewpoint of Christ who overcame temptation. Turning away bread is not so much about fasting as it is about recognizing that there is more to life than food. Our god is not the belly. When we come to the end of our lives, what will we have? With the power of Christ, let us overcome the temptation to see the value of our lives only in terms of the world. Instead, may we see with the eyes of faith that human relationships are good in and of themselves. Bonds formed in this way last through life eternal.

Connecting the Responsorial Psalm to the Readings

Today's psalm presents us with two truths: as human beings our relationship with God and others is marked by sin in some way, and God's mercy is great enough to wipe out the effects of sin and wash away all guilt. The second reading from St. Paul's letter to the Romans interprets the story of our first parents' sin saying, "[T]hrough one transgression / condemnation came upon us all." And then continues, referencing Jesus' victory over sin and death: "[S]o, through one righteous act, / acquittal and life came to all."

Psalmist Preparation

In this season of Lent how are you being called to live deeply into the truth of your own sinfulness and the truth of God's overwhelming mercy?

Prayer

Free us, O God, from the temptation
of not believing in our hearts what we sing with our mouths,
for the Word you speak is living bread for the hungry.
O Lord, open my lips,
and my mouth shall proclaim your praise. Amen.

MARCH 8, 2020

Gospel (Matt 17:1-9; L25A)

Jesus took Peter, James, and John his brother, and led them up a high mountain by themselves. And he was transfigured before them; his face shone like the sun and his clothes became white as light. And behold, Moses and Elijah appeared to them, conversing with him. Then Peter said to Jesus in reply, "Lord, it is good that we are here. If you wish, I will make three tents here, one for you, one for Moses, and one for Elijah." While he was still speaking, behold, a bright cloud cast a shadow over them, then from the cloud came a voice that said, "This

is my beloved Son, with whom I am well pleased; listen to him." When the disciples heard this, they fell prostrate and were very much afraid. But Jesus came and touched them, saying, "Rise, and do not be afraid." And when the disciples raised their eyes, they saw no one else but Jesus alone.

As they were coming down from the mountain, Jesus charged them, "Do not tell the vision to anyone until the Son of Man has been raised from the dead."

First Reading (Gen 12:1-4a)

The LORD said to Abram: "Go forth from the land of your kinsfolk and from your father's house to a land that I will show you.

"I will make of you a great nation,
   and I will bless you;
I will make your name great,
   so that you will be a blessing.
I will bless those who bless you
   and curse those who curse you.
All the communities of the earth
   shall find blessing in you."

Abram went as the LORD directed him.

Responsorial Psalm (Ps 33:4-5, 18-19, 20, 22)

R̂. (22) Lord, let your mercy be on us, as we place our trust in you.

Upright is the word of the LORD,
  and all his works are trustworthy.
He loves justice and right;
  of the kindness of the LORD the earth is full.

R̂. Lord, let your mercy be on us, as we place our trust in you.

See, the eyes of the LORD are upon those who fear him,
  upon those who hope for his kindness,
to deliver them from death
  and preserve them in spite of famine.

R̂. Lord, let your mercy be on us, as we place our trust in you.

Our soul waits for the LORD,
  who is our help and our shield.
May your kindness, O LORD, be upon us
  who have put our hope in you.

R̂. Lord, let your mercy be on us, as we place our trust in you.

See Appendix, p. 204, for Second Reading

Reflecting on Living the Gospel

The transfiguration of Jesus surely emboldened the disciples in their faith, while it also seized them with fear. This mountaintop experience meant even more after the resurrection when the words of Jesus became clear. The gospel today reminds us of our ultimate end, which is to be with Jesus in the heavenly realm. With such knowledge, cares of the world may wash away. Even a desire to commemorate such an event, as Peter desired to build three tents, is as nothing when compared to the experience itself. We have a foreshadowing of eternal glory.

Connecting the Responsorial Psalm to the Readings

Today's responsorial psalm paints a picture of God's mercy placed upon us, almost as if we could wear it as a cloak or shield. In the transfiguration, Jesus appears to Peter, James, and John in clothing as "white as light." We might consider the event in our own lives when we, too, wore clothing that covered us in the light of God. In the white baptismal garment we were proclaimed "a new creation" clothed in Christ.

Psalmist Preparation

As we continue journeying toward the feast of Easter and the moment when we renew our own baptismal promises, how do you experience yourself as clothed in the mercy and love of Christ?

Prayer

Lord, it is good that we are here to sing your praise.
But teach us to follow you even to the cross
that not by works but by your grace we may be saved.
Let your mercy be on us, O God,
as we place our trust in you. Amen.

***Gospel* (John 4:5-42**
[or shorter form below John 4:5-15, 19b-26, 39a, 40-42]; L28A)

Jesus came to a town of Samaria called Sychar, near the plot of land that Jacob had given to his son Joseph. Jacob's well was there. Jesus, tired from his journey, sat down there at the well. It was about noon.

A woman of Samaria came to draw water. Jesus said to her, "Give me a drink." His disciples had gone into the town to buy food. The Samaritan woman said to him, "How can you, a Jew, ask me, a Samaritan woman, for a drink?" —For Jews use nothing in common with Samaritans.— Jesus answered and said to her, "If you knew the gift of God and who is saying to you, 'Give me a drink,' you would have asked him and he would have given you living water." The woman said to him, "Sir, you do not even have a bucket and the cistern is deep; where then can you get this living water? Are you greater than our father Jacob, who gave us this cistern and drank from it himself with his children and his flocks?" Jesus answered and said to her, "Everyone who drinks this water will be thirsty again; but whoever drinks the water I shall give will never thirst; the water I shall give will become in him a spring of water welling up to eternal life." The woman said to him, "Sir, give me this water, so that I may not be thirsty or have to keep coming here to draw water."

"I can see that you are a prophet. Our ancestors worshiped on this mountain; but you people say that the place to worship is in Jerusalem." Jesus said to her, "Believe me, woman, the hour is coming when you will worship the Father neither on this mountain nor in Jerusalem. You people worship what you do not understand; we worship what we understand, because salvation is from the Jews. But the hour is coming, and is now here, when true worshipers will worship the Father in Spirit and truth; and indeed the Father seeks such people to worship him. God is Spirit, and those who worship him must worship in Spirit and truth." The woman said to him, "I know that the Messiah is coming, the one called the Christ; when he comes, he will tell us everything." Jesus said to her, "I am he, the one who is speaking with you."

Many of the Samaritans of that town began to believe in him. When the Samaritans came to him, they invited him to stay with them; and he stayed there two days. Many more began to believe in him because of his word, and they said to the woman, "We no longer believe because of your word; for we have heard for ourselves, and we know that this is truly the savior of the world."

First Reading (Exod 17:3-7)

In those days, in their thirst for water, the people grumbled against Moses, saying, "Why did you ever make us leave Egypt? Was it just to have us die here of thirst with our children and our livestock?" So Moses cried out to the LORD, "What shall I do with this people? A little more and they will stone me!" The LORD answered Moses, "Go over there in front of the people, along with some of the elders of Israel, holding in your hand, as you go, the staff with which you struck the river. I will be standing there in front of you on the rock in Horeb. Strike the rock, and the water will flow from it for the people to drink." This Moses did, in the presence of the elders of Israel. The place was called Massah and Meribah, because the Israelites quarreled there and tested the LORD, saying, "Is the LORD in our midst or not?"

Responsorial Psalm (Ps 95:1-2, 6-7, 8-9)

R̸. (8) If today you hear his voice, harden not your hearts.

Come, let us sing joyfully to the LORD;
  let us acclaim the Rock of our salvation.
Let us come into his presence with thanksgiving;
  let us joyfully sing psalms to him.

R̸. If today you hear his voice, harden not your hearts.

Come, let us bow down in worship;
  let us kneel before the LORD who made us.
For he is our God,
  and we are the people he shepherds, the flock he guides.

R̸. If today you hear his voice, harden not your hearts.

Oh, that today you would hear his voice:
  "Harden not your hearts as at Meribah,
  as in the day of Massah in the desert,
where your fathers tempted me;
  they tested me though they had seen my works."

R̸. If today you hear his voice, harden not your hearts.

See Appendix, p. 204, for Second Reading

Reflecting on Living the Gospel

Each of us came to faith through someone else. The woman at the well shared her experience with the townspeople. Many believed upon hearing, and many more heard for themselves and believed. Even the process of believing or, rather, coming to faith is gradual. Terms like "prophet" give way to "Christ" and ultimately (in this story) to "Savior." Jesus cannot be encapsulated by one title or in one encounter. The initial experience leaves the woman and the townspeople wanting more. Such is the life of faith. We do not have a once-and-for-all encounter. But a relationship with Jesus unfolds over time, ever deepening, ever revealing, until we ultimately encounter the cross and the exaltation.

Connecting the Responsorial Psalm to the Readings

Within the book of Psalms there are many places that use the imagery of a shepherd and sheep. In today's psalm we hear ourselves proclaimed as "the people [God] shepherds, the flock he guides." In the most beloved psalm about God as a shepherd (Psalm 23), we are told how we are cared by for the Lord: "In green pastures he makes me lie down; / to still waters he leads me; / he restores my soul" (23:2-3; NABRE). This is the same shepherd who produces water from a rock to satisfy the thirst of the Israelites on their journey to the Promised Land, and also the shepherd in today's gospel where Jesus tells the Samaritan woman that he is the source of living water, the only water that can quench thirst forever.

Psalmist Preparation

Within a flock the sheep must know and follow the voice of their shepherd, lest they wander away from safety. How do you live out your relationship to God, the shepherd? Where do you hear his voice calling to you at this moment in your life?

Prayer

Lord Jesus, you are truly the Savior of the world.
Soften our hardened hearts in the springs of eternal life
that we may hear your word and announce your salvation.
Come, let us sing joyfully to the Lord;
let us acclaim the Rock of our salvation. Amen.

Gospel (John 9:1-41 [or shorter form below John 9:1, 6-9, 13-17, 34-38]; L31A)

As Jesus passed by he saw a man blind from birth. He spat on the ground and made clay with the saliva, and smeared the clay on his eyes, and said to him, "Go wash in the Pool of Siloam"—which means Sent—. So he went and washed, and came back able to see.

His neighbors and those who had seen him earlier as a beggar said, "Isn't this the one who used to sit and beg?" Some said, "It is," but others said, "No, he just looks like him." He said, "I am."

They brought the one who was once blind to the Pharisees. Now Jesus had made clay and opened his eyes on a sabbath. So then the Pharisees also asked him how he was able to see. He said to them, "He put clay on my eyes, and I washed, and now I can see." So some of the Pharisees said, "This man is not from God, because he does not keep the sabbath." But others said, "How can a sinful man do such signs?" And there was a division among them. So they said to the blind man again, "What do you have to say about him, since he opened your eyes?" He said, "He is a prophet."

They answered and said to him, "You were born totally in sin, and are you trying to teach us?" Then they threw him out.

When Jesus heard that they had thrown him out, he found him and said, "Do you believe in the Son of Man?" He answered and said, "Who is he, sir, that I may believe in him?" Jesus said to him, "You have seen him, and the one speaking with you is he." He said, "I do believe, Lord," and he worshiped him.

First Reading (1 Sam 16:1b, 6-7, 10-13a)

The LORD said to Samuel: "Fill your horn with oil, and be on your way. I am sending you to Jesse of Bethlehem, for I have chosen my king from among his sons."

As Jesse and his sons came to the sacrifice, Samuel looked at Eliab and thought, "Surely the LORD's anointed is here before him." But the LORD said to Samuel: "Do not judge from his appearance or from his lofty stature, because I have rejected him. Not as man sees does God see, because man sees the appearance but the Lord looks into the heart." In the same way Jesse presented seven sons before Samuel, but Samuel said to Jesse, "The Lord has not chosen any one of these." Then Samuel asked Jesse, "Are these all the sons you have?" Jesse replied, "There is still the youngest, who is tending the sheep." Samuel said to Jesse, "Send for him; we will not begin the sacrificial banquet until he arrives here." Jesse sent and had the young man brought to them. He was ruddy, a youth handsome to behold and making a splendid appearance. The Lord said, "There—anoint him, for this is the one!" Then Samuel, with the horn of oil in hand, anointed David in the presence of his brothers; and from that day on, the spirit of the Lord rushed upon David.

Responsorial Psalm (Ps 23:1-3a, 3b-4, 5, 6)

R̷. (1) The Lord is my shepherd; there is nothing I shall want.

The Lord is my shepherd; I shall not want.
  In verdant pastures he gives me repose;
beside restful waters he leads me;
  he refreshes my soul.

R̷. The Lord is my shepherd; there is nothing I shall want.

He guides me in right paths
  for his name's sake.
Even though I walk in the dark valley
  I fear no evil; for you are at my side
with your rod and your staff
  that give me courage.

R̷. The Lord is my shepherd; there is nothing I shall want.

You spread the table before me
  in the sight of my foes;
you anoint my head with oil;
  my cup overflows.

R̷. The Lord is my shepherd; there is nothing I shall want.

Only goodness and kindness follow me
  all the days of my life;
and I shall dwell in the house of the Lord
  for years to come.

R̷. The Lord is my shepherd; there is nothing I shall want.

See Appendix, p. 204, for Second Reading

Reflecting on Living the Gospel

Jesus heals the man born blind. The story is masterfully and artfully complex yet succinct. Drama abounds and intrigue develops with each verse. Fundamental themes and metaphors such as light versus darkness, sight versus blindness, knowing versus not knowing, and more, including willful ignorance in the face of demonstrable evidence, are woven together in this gospel passage that is the source of tremendous insight and wisdom. Jesus takes the initiative. He creates cognitive dissonance in the minds and hearts of many, demanding that they make a decision for or against him. When do we face such encounters with Christ? What is our response?

Connecting the Responsorial Psalm to the Readings

David is called in from the fields where he is tending the sheep to be presented to Samuel, who anoints his head with oil that marks him as the next king of Israel. Tradition tells us that David, the shepherd, penned today's psalm to God, the ultimate Shepherd, who watches over and anoints all his sheep with his tender care. On the day of our baptism, we were anointed with the oil of salvation and claimed as Christ's own. The second reading from St. Paul harkens to baptism as well with his commandment to the Ephesians: "Live as children of light."

Psalmist Preparation

Throughout the season of Lent we journey with the catechumens toward baptism and the renewal of our own baptismal promises. How do you strive to live as a child of light and an anointed one of God?

Prayer

Lord Jesus, you are the Light of the world.
Anoint our eyes with your merciful gaze
that we may be healed of our blindness and see one another with your love.
The Lord is my shepherd;
there is nothing I shall want. Amen.

Gospel (John 11:1-45 [or shorter form below John 11:3-7, 17, 20-27, 33b-45]; L34A)

The sisters of Lazarus sent word to Jesus saying, "Master, the one you love is ill." When Jesus heard this he said, "This illness is not to end in death, but is for the glory of God, that the Son of God may be glorified through it." Now Jesus loved Martha and her sister and Lazarus. So when he heard that he was ill, he remained for two days in the place where he was. Then after this he said to his disciples, "Let us go back to Judea."

When Jesus arrived, he found that Lazarus had already been in the tomb for four days. When Martha heard that Jesus was coming, she went to meet him; but Mary sat at home. Martha said to Jesus, "Lord, if you had been here, my brother would not have died. But even now I know that whatever you ask of God, God will give you." Jesus said to her, "Your brother will rise." Martha said, "I know he will rise, in the resurrection on the last day." Jesus told her, "I am the resurrection and the life; whoever believes in me, even if he dies, will live, and everyone who lives and believes in me will never die. Do you believe this?" She said to him, "Yes, Lord. I have come to believe that you are the Christ, the Son of God, the one who is coming into the world."

He became perturbed and deeply troubled, and said, "Where have you laid him?" They said to him, "Sir, come and see." And Jesus wept. So the Jews said, "See how he loved him." But some of them said, "Could not the one who opened the eyes of the blind man have done something so that this man would not have died?"

So Jesus, perturbed again, came to the tomb. It was a cave, and a stone lay across it. Jesus said, "Take away the stone." Martha, the dead man's sister, said to him, "Lord, by now there will be a stench; he has been dead for four days." Jesus said to her, "Did I not tell you that if you believe you will see the glory of God?" So they took away the stone. And Jesus raised his eyes and said, "Father, I thank you for hearing me. I know that you always hear me; but because of the crowd here I have said this, that they may believe that you sent me." And when he had said this, he cried out in a loud voice, "Lazarus, come out!" The dead man came out, tied hand and foot with burial bands, and his face was wrapped in a cloth. So Jesus said to them, "Untie him and let him go."

Now many of the Jews who had come to Mary and seen what he had done began to believe in him.

First Reading (Ezek 37:12-14)

Thus says the Lord GOD: O my people, I will open your graves and have you rise from them, and bring you back to the land of Israel. Then you shall know that I am the LORD, when I open your graves and have you rise from them, O my people! I will put my spirit in you that you may live, and I will settle you upon your land; thus you shall know that I am the LORD. I have promised, and I will do it, says the LORD.

Responsorial Psalm (Ps 130:1-2, 3-4, 5-6, 7-8)

℞. (7) With the Lord there is mercy and fullness of redemption.

Out of the depths I cry to you, O LORD;
    LORD, hear my voice!
Let your ears be attentive
    to my voice in supplication.

℞. With the Lord there is mercy and fullness of redemption.

If you, O LORD, mark iniquities,
    LORD, who can stand?
But with you is forgiveness,
    that you may be revered.

℞. With the Lord there is mercy and fullness of redemption.

I trust in the LORD;
    my soul trusts in his word.
More than sentinels wait for the dawn,
    let Israel wait for the LORD.

℞. With the Lord there is mercy and fullness of redemption.

For with the LORD is kindness
    and with him is plenteous redemption;
and he will redeem Israel
    from all their iniquities.

℞. With the Lord there is mercy and fullness of redemption.

See Appendix, p. 204, for Second Reading

Reflecting on Living the Gospel

After Jesus raised Lazarus from the dead, many began to believe in him—that he had been sent by the Father. What do we believe about Jesus? Do we believe he is the author of life with power over death? Are there any people like Lazarus in our own lives who need to be raised to new life? Lazarus was a prefiguring of the resurrection. And yet, even Lazarus died again. Jesus' own resurrection is not a mere resuscitation, but a raising to new life, qualitatively different, never subject to death again.

Connecting the Responsorial Psalm to the Readings

Again, as in the First and Second Sundays of Lent, our responsorial psalm emphasizes God's mercy and power to redeem. Our hope in this mercy and redemption is to rival that of a "sentinel [waiting] for the dawn." What an apt image for our trust and belief in the one who promises to call us forth from our graves and offers us resurrected life in the face of death. Like a sentinel, we might at times grow weary in the watches of the night, and yet, we know that the dawn will break again and bring us into the light of a new day.

Psalmist Preparation

In today's gospel Jesus tells Martha, "I am the resurrection and the life; / whoever believes in me, even if he dies, will live, / and everyone who lives and believes in me will never die. / Do you believe this?" What would your response to this question be?

Prayer

Lord Jesus, you are the resurrection and the life.
Still you weep with us when we weep at death's door.
Strengthen our faith to believe in you always.
I trust in the Lord;
my soul trusts in God's word. Amen.

Gospel at the procession with palms
(Matt 21:1-11; L37A)

Gospel at Mass **(Matt 26:14–27:66 [or 27:11-54]; L38A)**

First Reading **(Isa 50:4-7)**

The Lord God has given me
    a well-trained tongue,
that I might know how to speak to
        the weary
    a word that will rouse them.
Morning after morning
    he opens my ear that I may hear;
and I have not rebelled,
    have not turned back.
I gave my back to those who beat me,
    my cheeks to those who plucked my beard;
my face I did not shield
    from buffets and spitting.

The Lord God is my help,
    therefore I am not disgraced;
I have set my face like flint,
    knowing that I shall not be put to shame.

Responsorial Psalm **(Ps 22:8-9, 17-18, 19-20, 23-24)**

℞. (2a) My God, my God, why have you abandoned me?

All who see me scoff at me;
    they mock me with parted lips, they wag their heads:
"He relied on the Lord; let him deliver him,
    let him rescue him, if he loves him."

℞. My God, my God, why have you abandoned me?

Indeed, many dogs surround me,
    a pack of evildoers closes in upon me;
they have pierced my hands and my feet;
    I can count all my bones.

℞. My God, my God, why have you abandoned me?

They divide my garments among them,
and for my vesture they cast lots.
But you, O Lord, be not far from me;
O my help, hasten to aid me.

R̸. My God, my God, why have you abandoned me?

I will proclaim your name to my brethren;
in the midst of the assembly I will praise you:
"You who fear the Lord, praise him;
all you descendants of Jacob, give glory to him;
revere him, all you descendants of Israel!"

R̸. My God, my God, why have you abandoned me?

See Appendix, p. 204, for Second Reading

Reflecting on Living the Gospel

Palm Sunday is a commemoration of highs and lows, exaltation and tragedy. We enter the church bearing palms, singing Hosanna, and only minutes later we cry in unison, "Let him be crucified." The liturgical juxtaposition is certainly intended and representative of fickle humanity, not only during the events of Holy Week, but quite regularly, down into our modern era. Profound themes of betrayal, trust, friendship, power, and humility are present in the gospel reading from Matthew. The example of Jesus inspires us to be true to God's will in our own lives. We are called to remain faithful to God, ever trusting in his wisdom and providential care.

Connecting the Responsorial Psalm to the Readings

In our readings for today we go from the crowd's triumphant shouts of "Hosanna" to the silence of the tomb where Jesus' body is placed. We find the same contrast of triumph and despair in today's psalm, which begins "My God, my God, why have you abandoned me?" and ends with the psalmist calling on the assembly and all the descendants of Israel to praise the Lord and "give glory to him."

Psalmist Preparation

Within the psalms we find all human emotions brought to God, from anger and despair, to love and trust. In Jesus' birth, life, death, and resurrection, God enters into the fullness of human emotion. We need not be afraid to bring all of who we are to our loving Father.

Prayer

As we enter the Mystery of this sacred time,
grant us, Lord, a well-trained tongue,
that we might speak and sing a word to rouse the weary heart.
I will proclaim your name to my people;
in the midst of the assembly I will praise you. Amen.
and to the glory beyond. We ask this in his name. Amen.

Gospel (John 13:1-15; L39ABC)

Before the feast of Passover, Jesus knew that his hour had come to pass from this world to the Father. He loved his own in the world and he loved them to the end. The devil had already induced Judas, son of Simon the Iscariot, to hand him over. So, during supper, fully aware that the Father had put everything into his power and that he had come from God and was returning to God, he rose

from supper and took off his outer garments. He took a towel and tied it around his waist. Then he poured water into a basin and began to wash the disciples' feet and dry them with the towel around his waist. He came to Simon Peter, who said to him, "Master, are you going to wash my feet?" Jesus answered and said to him, "What I am doing, you do not understand now, but you will understand later." Peter said to him, "You will never wash my feet." Jesus answered him, "Unless I wash you, you will have no inheritance with me." Simon Peter said to him, "Master, then not only my feet, but my hands and head as well." Jesus said to him, "Whoever has bathed has no need except to have his feet washed, for he is clean all over; so you are clean, but not all." For he knew who would betray him; for this reason, he said, "Not all of you are clean."

So when he had washed their feet and put his garments back on and reclined at table again, he said to them, "Do you realize what I have done for you? You call me 'teacher' and 'master,' and rightly so, for indeed I am. If I, therefore, the master and teacher, have washed your feet, you ought to wash one another's feet. I have given you a model to follow, so that as I have done for you, you should also do."

First Reading (Exod 12:1-8, 11-14)

The LORD said to Moses and Aaron in the land of Egypt, "This month shall stand at the head of your calendar; you shall reckon it the first month of the year. Tell the whole community of Israel: On the tenth of this month every one of your families must procure for itself a lamb, one apiece for each household. If a family is too small for a whole lamb, it shall join the nearest household in procuring one and shall share in the lamb in proportion to the number of persons who partake of it. The lamb must be a year-old male and without blemish. You may take it from either the sheep or the goats. You shall keep it until the fourteenth day of this month, and then, with the whole assembly of Israel present, it shall be slaughtered during the evening twilight. They shall take some of its blood and apply it to the two doorposts and the lintel of every house in which they partake of the lamb. That same night they shall eat its roasted flesh with unleavened bread and bitter herbs.

"This is how you are to eat it: with your loins girt, sandals on your feet and your staff in hand, you shall eat like those who are in flight. It is the Passover of the LORD. For on this same night I will go through Egypt, striking down every firstborn of the land, both man and beast, and executing judgment on all the gods of Egypt—I, the LORD! But the blood will mark the houses where you are. Seeing the blood, I will pass over you; thus, when I strike the land of Egypt, no destructive blow will come upon you.

"This day shall be a memorial feast for you, which all your generations shall celebrate with pilgrimage to the LORD, as a perpetual institution."

Responsorial Psalm (Ps 116:12-13, 15-16bc, 17-18)

R℣. (cf. 1 Cor 10:16) Our blessing-cup is a communion with the Blood of Christ.

How shall I make a return to the LORD
    for all the good he has done for me?
The cup of salvation I will take up,
    and I will call upon the name of the LORD.

R℣. Our blessing-cup is a communion with the Blood of Christ.

Precious in the eyes of the LORD
    is the death of his faithful ones.
I am your servant, the son of your handmaid;
    you have loosed my bonds.

R℣. Our blessing-cup is a communion with the Blood of Christ.

To you will I offer sacrifice of thanksgiving,
    and I will call upon the name of the LORD.
My vows to the LORD I will pay
    in the presence of all his people.

R℣. Our blessing-cup is a communion with the Blood of Christ.

See Appendix, p. 205, for Second Reading

Reflecting on Living the Gospel

As we begin to commemorate these sacred days, we call to mind the essential element of Christian identity, which is service. Perhaps more than prayer, liturgy, or other identifiable markers of our faith, we are called to imitate Jesus in service to others. As master, Jesus was not content to be served, but to serve. So let us, too, look for opportunities to be of service to our family, neighbors, friends, fellow parishioners, and any others who may need our help.

Connecting the Responsorial Psalm to the Readings

The first verse of today's psalm asks, "How shall I make a return to the LORD / for all the good he has done for me?" On Holy Thursday, we commemorate and participate in a particular way in the Lord's Supper when Jesus commanded his closest friends, "Do this in remembrance of me." As we draw near to the altar table at each eucharistic celebration, we hear the words proclaimed again, "The Body of Christ. The Blood of Christ." When we respond, "Amen," we are not only affirming the true presence of Jesus, but also confirming our own deepest vocation, to be the bread that is broken and the wine that is poured out for the sake of others.

Psalmist Preparation

In your life of faith, how do you "make a return" to God for the blessings you have been given?

Prayer

You give us a new commandment, Lord,
to love one another as you loved us.
May your paschal mystery shape us ever more into your likeness.
Let us offer our sacrifice of praise
for all the good God has done for us. Amen.

Gospel (John 18:1–19:42; L40ABC)

First Reading (Isa 52:13–53:12)

See, my servant shall prosper,
   he shall be raised high and greatly
      exalted.
Even as many were amazed at him—
   so marred was his look beyond
      human semblance
   and his appearance beyond that of
      the sons of man—
so shall he startle many nations,
   because of him kings shall stand speechless;
for those who have not been told shall see,
   those who have not heard shall ponder it.

Who would believe what we have heard?
   To whom has the arm of the LORD been revealed?
He grew up like a sapling before him,
   like a shoot from the parched earth;
there was in him no stately bearing to make us look at him,
   nor appearance that would attract us to him.
He was spurned and avoided by people,
   a man of suffering, accustomed to infirmity,
one of those from whom people hide their faces,
   spurned, and we held him in no esteem.

Yet it was our infirmities that he bore,
   our sufferings that he endured,
while we thought of him as stricken,
   as one smitten by God and afflicted.
But he was pierced for our offenses,
   crushed for our sins;
upon him was the chastisement that makes us whole,
   by his stripes we were healed.
We had all gone astray like sheep,
   each following his own way;
but the LORD laid upon him
   the guilt of us all.

Though he was harshly treated, he submitted
   and opened not his mouth;
like a lamb led to the slaughter
   or a sheep before the shearers,
   he was silent and opened not his mouth.
Oppressed and condemned, he was taken away,
   and who would have thought any more of his destiny?
When he was cut off from the land of the living,
   and smitten for the sin of his people,
a grave was assigned him among the wicked
   and a burial place with evildoers,
though he had done no wrong
   nor spoken any falsehood.
But the LORD was pleased
   to crush him in infirmity.

If he gives his life as an offering for sin,
   he shall see his descendants in a long life,
   and the will of the LORD shall be accomplished through him.

Because of his affliction
   he shall see the light
     in fullness of days;
through his suffering, my servant shall justify many,
   and their guilt he shall bear.
Therefore I will give him his portion among the great,
   and he shall divide the spoils with the mighty,
because he surrendered himself to death
   and was counted among the wicked;
and he shall take away the sins of many,
   and win pardon for their offenses.

Responsorial Psalm (Ps 31:2, 6, 12-13, 15-16, 17, 25)

R̊. (Luke 23:46) Father, into your hands I commend my spirit.

In you, O LORD, I take refuge;
   let me never be put to shame.
In your justice rescue me.
Into your hands I commend my spirit;
   you will redeem me, O LORD, O faithful God.

℞. Father, into your hands I commend my spirit.

For all my foes I am an object of reproach,
  a laughingstock to my neighbors, and a dread to my friends;
  they who see me abroad flee from me.
I am forgotten like the unremembered dead;
  I am like a dish that is broken.

℞. Father, into your hands I commend my spirit.

But my trust is in you, O LORD;
  I say, "You are my God.
In your hands is my destiny; rescue me
  from the clutches of my enemies and my persecutors."

℞. Father, into your hands I commend my spirit.

Let your face shine upon your servant;
  save me in your kindness.
Take courage and be stouthearted,
  all you who hope in the LORD.

℞. Father, into your hands I commend my spirit.

See Appendix, p. 205, for Second Reading

Reflecting on Living the Gospel

Jesus' own example in the face of hatred, violence, false accusation, and ultimately death is to be true to himself without responding in kind. It can be a challenge to follow that model in our own lives when the inclination is to strike back when struck or to fight fire with fire. But in a world beaten down by injustice, cruelty, systems of oppression, and general inequity, our faith is in a higher power. In God's kingdom the oppressed in this world will reign and the oppressors will be brought low. Confident of this outcome, we align ourselves with Jesus, with the poor, and with the oppressed.

Connecting the Responsorial Psalm to the Readings

Today's psalm (taken from Isaiah) contains the last words Jesus speaks before perishing on the cross in Luke's gospel, "into your hands I commend my spirit" (Luke 23:46; NABRE). On Good Friday we read from the passion according to John. In John's account, Jesus takes a sip of wine, says, "It is finished," and then, "bowing his head, he handed over the spirit." In both gospels, we see Jesus, calm and resolute in the face of death, truly laying down his life as he said he would (John 10:18). And yet we know that it isn't for the sake of death itself, but for the resurrection that this event takes place. As Isaiah reminds us in the responsorial psalm, the one who gives up all to God, including his very spirit, will be redeemed.

Psalmist Preparation

Today's psalm ends with the admonition, "Take courage and be stouthearted, / all of you who hope in the LORD." Where are you being called upon to be courageous in the sure hope that life is stronger than death and light stronger than darkness?

Prayer

Out of love for us, O God,
your Son gave his life on a cross
and made it the throne of grace and mercy for all.
Into your hands, Father, we place our lives.
Let us trust and hope in the Lord, our God. Amen.
Additional readings can be found in the Lectionary for Mass.

APRIL 11, 2020

*Additional readings can be found
in the Lectionary for Mass.*

Gospel (Matt 28:1-10; L41ABC)

After the sabbath, as the first day of the
week was dawning, Mary Magdalene
and the other Mary came to see the
tomb. And behold, there was a great
earthquake; for an angel of the Lord descended from heaven, approached, rolled
back the stone, and sat upon it. His appearance was like lightning and his

clothing was white as snow. The guards were shaken with fear of him
and became like dead men. Then the angel said to the women in reply,
"Do not be afraid! I know that you are seeking Jesus the crucified. He is
not here, for he has been raised just as he said. Come and see the place
where he lay. Then go quickly and tell his disciples, 'He has been raised
from the dead, and he is going before you to Galilee; there you will see
him.' Behold, I have told you." Then they went away quickly from the
tomb, fearful yet overjoyed, and ran to announce this to his disciples. And
behold, Jesus met them on their way and greeted them. They approached,
embraced his feet, and did him homage. Then Jesus said to them, "Do not
be afraid. Go tell my brothers to go to Galilee, and there they will see me."

Epistle (Rom 6:3-11)

Brothers and sisters: Are you unaware that we who were baptized into
Christ Jesus were baptized into his death? We were indeed buried with
him through baptism into death, so that, just as Christ was raised from
the dead by the glory of the Father, we too might live in newness of life.

For if we have grown into union with him through a death like his, we
shall also be united with him in the resurrection. We know that our old
self was crucified with him, so that our sinful body might be done away
with, that we might no longer be in slavery to sin. For a dead person has
been absolved from sin. If, then, we have died with Christ, we believe that
we shall also live with him. We know that Christ, raised from the dead,
dies no more; death no longer has power over him. As to his death, he
died to sin once and for all; as to his life, he lives for God. Consequently,
you too must think of yourselves as being dead to sin and living for God
in Christ Jesus.

Responsorial Psalm (Ps 118:1-2, 16-17, 22-23)

R℣. Alleluia, alleluia, alleluia.

Give thanks to the LORD, for he is good,
    for his mercy endures forever.
Let the house of Israel say,
    "His mercy endures forever."

R℣. Alleluia, alleluia, alleluia.

"The right hand of the LORD has struck with power;
    the right hand of the LORD is exalted.
I shall not die, but live,
    and declare the works of the LORD."

R℣. Alleluia, alleluia, alleluia.

The stone which the builders rejected
    has become the cornerstone.
By the LORD has this been done;
    it is wonderful in our eyes.

R℣. Alleluia, alleluia, alleluia.

Reflecting on Living the Gospel

Women, Mary Magdalene and the other Mary, were the recipients of the first risen appearance, according to Matthew. They are told to relate the good news to the others—that Jesus is risen and they will see him in Galilee. Here it is not Peter or the Beloved Disciple, or the other disciples, who witness Jesus first. Mary Magdalene and the other Mary have that distinction. Jesus chooses those whom he wills. And we, too, are witness to his presence in the world. The mission of the women is our mission: proclaim the good news to others.

Connecting the Responsorial Psalm to the Readings

We have arrived at the holiest night of our church year. What better way to celebrate and keep vigil than by entering into the story of our salvation told through the Scriptures? The psalms for tonight recall what the Lord has done ("fixed the earth upon its foundation," "covered himself in glory," "rescued me") and calls upon God to do it yet again ("renew the face of the earth," "show me the path to life," "[s]end forth your light and your fidelity"). It has been said that liturgy is a place in which we live "between memory and hope," and nowhere is that more apparent than at the Easter Vigil.

Psalmist Preparation

As you prepare to lead the assembly in lifting their voices to God, take a moment to consider memory and hope in your own journey of faith. What wonders has God done in your own life? What are you hoping for now?

Prayer

Rejoice, heavenly powers:
Choirs of angels sing!
Let trumpets of salvation sound:
Choirs of angels sing!
The gloom of darkness is banished away:
For Christ has broken the chains of death!
Let this holy church resound with joy!
For Christ has broken the chains of death! Amen.

Gospel (John 20:1-9; L42ABC)

On the first day of the week, Mary of
Magdala came to the tomb early in the
morning, while it was still dark, and
saw the stone removed from the tomb.
So she ran and went to Simon Peter and
to the other disciple whom Jesus loved,
and told them, "They have taken the
Lord from the tomb, and we don't know
where they put him." So Peter and the
other disciple went out and came to the

tomb. They both ran, but the other disciple ran faster than Peter and arrived at the tomb first; he bent down and saw the burial cloths there, but
did not go in. When Simon Peter arrived after him, he went into the tomb
and saw the burial cloths there, and the cloth that had covered his head,
not with the burial cloths but rolled up in a separate place. Then the
other disciple also went in, the one who had arrived at the tomb first, and
he saw and believed. For they did not yet understand the Scripture that
he had to rise from the dead.

or Gospel (Matt 28:1-10; L41A)

or at an afternoon or evening Mass
Gospel (Luke 24:13-35; L46)

First Reading (Acts 10:34a, 37-43)

Peter proceeded to speak and said: "You know what has happened all over
Judea, beginning in Galilee after the baptism that John preached, how
God anointed Jesus of Nazareth with the Holy Spirit and power. He went
about doing good and healing all those oppressed by the devil, for God
was with him. We are witnesses of all that he did both in the country of
the Jews and in Jerusalem. They put him to death by hanging him on a
tree. This man God raised on the third day and granted that he be visible,
not to all the people, but to us, the witnesses chosen by God in advance,
who ate and drank with him after he rose from the dead. He commis-
sioned us to preach to the people and testify that he is the one appointed
by God as judge of the living and the dead. To him all the prophets bear
witness, that everyone who believes in him will receive forgiveness of
sins through his name."

Responsorial Psalm (Ps 118:1-2, 16-17, 22-23)

℟. (24) This is the day the Lord has made; let us rejoice and be glad.
or: ℟. Alleluia.

Give thanks to the LORD, for he is good,
for his mercy endures forever.
Let the house of Israel say,
"His mercy endures forever."

℟. This is the day the Lord has made; let us rejoice and be glad.
or: ℟. Alleluia.

"The right hand of the LORD has struck with power;
the right hand of the LORD is exalted.
I shall not die, but live,
and declare the works of the LORD."

℟. This is the day the Lord has made; let us rejoice and be glad.
or: ℟. Alleluia.

The stone which the builders rejected
has become the cornerstone.
By the LORD has this been done;
it is wonderful in our eyes.

℟. This is the day the Lord has made; let us rejoice and be glad.
or: ℟. Alleluia.

See Appendix, p. 205, for Second Reading

Reflecting on Living the Gospel

Much as it may sound surprising to us, the resurrection of Jesus seemed to be a surprise to his disciples. Mary of Magdala's first reaction is logical: the body was stolen. Peter and the Beloved Disciple see for themselves that the tomb is empty, but only one believes. They did not understand the Scripture. We are reminded that we live by faith and we seek understanding. Easter gives us our north star, the guiding light by which we live our lives. On this Easter morning, may we be open to the unexpected ways that God may work in our lives.

EASTER SUNDAY OF THE RESURRECTION

Connecting the Responsorial Psalm to the Readings

Throughout the Easter season there is the option to use "Alleluia" as the refrain for the responsorial psalm. After "fasting" from this word of pure joy for forty days, we now use it with great abandon in greetings, in hymns, and to hail the reading of the gospel. Today's psalm reminds us that this joy cannot be kept shrouded. It proclaims, "I shall not die, but live, / and declare the works of the LORD." In celebrating the resurrection of the Lord, this refrain becomes our own and our joy overflows.

Psalmist Preparation

In the Easter season, how do you embody joy in your words and actions?

Prayer

Christians, to the Paschal Lamb:
Sing your thankful praises!
The Prince of Life has conquered death:
Sing your thankful praises!
The empty tomb is filled with blessing:
Sing your thankful praises!
For Christ is risen! Alleluia! Alleluia!
Christ is risen indeed! Alleluia! Alleluia!

Gospel (John 20:19-31; L43A)

On the evening of that first day of the week, when the doors were locked, where the disciples were, for fear of the Jews, Jesus came and stood in their midst and said to them, "Peace be with you." When he had said this, he showed them his hands and his side. The disciples rejoiced when they saw the Lord. Jesus said to them again, "Peace be with you. As the Father has sent me, so I

send you." And when he had said this, he breathed on them and said to them, "Receive the Holy Spirit. Whose sins you forgive are forgiven them, and whose sins you retain are retained."

Thomas, called Didymus, one of the Twelve, was not with them when Jesus came. So the other disciples said to him, "We have seen the Lord." But he said to them, "Unless I see the mark of the nails in his hands and put my finger into the nailmarks and put my hand into his side, I will not believe."

Now a week later his disciples were again inside and Thomas was with them. Jesus came, although the doors were locked, and stood in their midst and said, "Peace be with you." Then he said to Thomas, "Put your finger here and see my hands, and bring your hand and put it into my side, and do not be unbelieving, but believe." Thomas answered and said to him, "My Lord and my God!" Jesus said to him, "Have you come to believe because you have seen me? Blessed are those who have not seen and have believed."

Now Jesus did many other signs in the presence of his disciples that are not written in this book. But these are written that you may come to believe that Jesus is the Christ, the Son of God, and that through this belief you may have life in his name.

First Reading (Acts 2:42-47)

They devoted themselves to the teaching of the apostles and to the communal life, to the breaking of bread and to the prayers. Awe came upon everyone, and many wonders and signs were done through the apostles. All who believed were together and had all things in common; they would sell their property and possessions and divide them among all according to each one's need. Every day they devoted themselves to meeting together in the temple area and to breaking bread in their homes. They ate their meals with exultation and sincerity of heart, praising God and enjoying favor with all the people. And every day the Lord added to their number those who were being saved.

Responsorial Psalm (Ps 118:2-4, 13-15, 22-24)

R℣. (1) Give thanks to the Lord for he is good, his love is everlasting.
or: R℣. Alleluia.

Let the house of Israel say,
   "His mercy endures forever."
Let the house of Aaron say,
   "His mercy endures forever."
Let those who fear the LORD say,
   "His mercy endures forever."

R℣. Give thanks to the Lord for he is good, his love is everlasting.
or: R℣. Alleluia.

I was hard pressed and was falling,
   but the LORD helped me.
My strength and my courage is the LORD,
   and he has been my savior.
The joyful shout of victory
   in the tents of the just.

R℣. Give thanks to the Lord for he is good, his love is everlasting.
or: R℣. Alleluia.

The stone which the builders rejected
   has become the cornerstone.
By the LORD has this been done;
   it is wonderful in our eyes.
This is the day the LORD has made;
   let us be glad and rejoice in it.

R℣. Give thanks to the Lord for he is good, his love is everlasting.
or: R℣. Alleluia.

See Appendix, p. 205, for Second Reading

Reflecting on Living the Gospel

On the evening of Easter Sunday, Jesus makes his appearance to the disciples, though Thomas is absent. It is only one week later when Jesus appears again. During this intervening week, what did the other disciples say to Thomas? Why was he obstinate in the face of their witness? Thomas experienced Jesus throughout his earthly ministry and heard the eyewitness testimony of his friends. Still, his lack of belief persisted. Only a personal experience of the risen Christ would melt away his doubt. Such is a model of how individuals come to faith. Sometimes, like Thomas, despite all the testimony of believers, faith does not take root unless one personally encounters the risen Christ.

Connecting the Responsorial Psalm to the Readings

This Second Sunday of Easter is also called Divine Mercy Sunday. In the gospel, Jesus encounters the disciples for the first time following their desertion of him during his passion and death. Instead of greeting them with reproach, he offers peace. The psalm for today also emphasizes the mercy of God. Three times in the first verse we hear the line repeated: "His mercy endures forever." Three is a number of fullness and completion in the Bible. As the responsorial proclaims, our God's love is everlasting.

Psalmist Preparation

As you prepare to proclaim the mercy of God to the assembly, consider where you have received this mercy in your own life. How do you live a life of mercy and forgiveness?

Prayer

Give thanks to the Lord, for God is good:
God's mercy endures forever!
Let all that has breath sing praise to God:
God's mercy endures forever!
God casts all fear and doubt away:
God's mercy endures forever!
Christ is risen! Alleluia! Alleluia!
Christ is risen indeed! Alleluia! Alleluia!

Gospel (Luke 24:13-35; L46A)

That very day, the first day of the week, two of Jesus' disciples were going to a village seven miles from Jerusalem called Emmaus, and they were conversing about all the things that had occurred. And it happened that while they were conversing and debating, Jesus himself drew near and walked with them, but their eyes were prevented from rec-

ognizing him. He asked them, "What are you discussing as you walk along?" They stopped, looking downcast. One of them, named Cleopas, said to him in reply, "Are you the only visitor to Jerusalem who does not know of the things that have taken place there in these days?" And he replied to them, "What sort of things?" They said to him, "The things that happened to Jesus the Nazarene, who was a prophet mighty in deed and word before God and all the people, how our chief priests and rulers both handed him over to a sentence of death and crucified him. But we were hoping that he would be the one to redeem Israel; and besides all this, it is now the third day since this took place. Some women from our group, however, have astounded us: they were at the tomb early in the morning and did not find his body; they came back and reported that they had indeed seen a vision of angels who announced that he was alive. Then some of those with us went to the tomb and found things just as the women had described, but him they did not see." And he said to them, "Oh, how foolish you are! How slow of heart to believe all that the prophets spoke! Was it not necessary that the Christ should suffer these things and enter into his glory?" Then beginning with Moses and all the prophets, he interpreted to them what referred to him in all the Scriptures. As they approached the village to which they were going, he gave the impression that he was going on farther. But they urged him, "Stay with us, for it is nearly evening and the day is almost over." So he went in to stay with them. And it happened that, while he was with them at table, he took bread, said the blessing, broke it, and gave it to them. With that their eyes were opened and they recognized him, but he vanished from their sight. Then they said to each other, "Were not our hearts burning within us while he spoke to us on the way and opened the Scriptures to us?" So they set out at once and returned to Jerusalem where they found gathered together the eleven and those with them who were saying, "The Lord has truly been raised and has appeared to Simon!" Then the two recounted what had taken place on the way and how he was made known to them in the breaking of bread.

First Reading (Acts 2:14, 22-33)

Then Peter stood up with the Eleven, raised his voice, and proclaimed: "You who are Jews, indeed all of you staying in Jerusalem. Let this be known to you, and listen to my words. You who are Israelites, hear these words. Jesus the Nazorean was a man commended to you by God with mighty deeds, wonders, and signs, which God worked through him in your midst, as you yourselves know. This man, delivered up by the set plan and foreknowledge of God, you killed, using lawless men to crucify him. But God raised him up, releasing him from the throes of death, because it was impossible for him to be held by it. For David says of him:

> *I saw the Lord ever before me,*
> *with him at my right hand I shall not be disturbed.*
> *Therefore my heart has been glad and my tongue has exulted;*
> *my flesh, too, will dwell in hope,*
> *because you will not abandon my soul to the netherworld,*
> *nor will you suffer your holy one to see corruption.*
> *You have made known to me the paths of life;*
> *you will fill me with joy in your presence.*

"My brothers, one can confidently say to you about the patriarch David that he died and was buried, and his tomb is in our midst to this day. But since he was a prophet and knew that God had sworn an oath to him that he would set one of his descendants upon his throne, he foresaw and spoke of the resurrection of the Christ, that neither was he abandoned to the netherworld nor did his flesh see corruption. God raised this Jesus; of this we are all witnesses. Exalted at the right hand of God, he received the promise of the Holy Spirit from the Father and poured him forth, as you see and hear."

Responsorial Psalm (Ps 16:1-2, 5, 7-8, 9-10, 11)

℟. (11a) Lord, you will show us the path of life. *or:* ℟. Alleluia.

Keep me, O God, for in you I take refuge;
  I say to the LORD, "My Lord are you."
O LORD, my allotted portion and my cup,
  you it is who hold fast my lot.

℟. Lord, you will show us the path of life. *or:* ℟. Alleluia.

I bless the LORD who counsels me;
  even in the night my heart exhorts me.
I set the LORD ever before me;
  with him at my right hand I shall not be disturbed.

℟. Lord, you will show us the path of life. *or:* ℟. Alleluia.

Therefore my heart is glad and my soul rejoices,
  my body, too, abides in confidence;
because you will not abandon my soul to the netherworld,
  nor will you suffer your faithful one to undergo corruption.

℟. Lord, you will show us the path of life. *or:* ℟. Alleluia.

You will show me the path to life,
  abounding joy in your presence,
  the delights at your right hand forever.

℟. Lord, you will show us the path of life. *or:* ℟. Alleluia.

See Appendix, p. 206, for Second Reading

Reflecting on Living the Gospel

After Easter, the disciples come to know Jesus in the breaking of the bread. He is present among his followers as he was prior to his death and resurrection, but now, he is present in a new way. Of course, as Catholics, we see this clearly in the Eucharist, when we take bread, bless it, break it, and give it. The bread broken is Christ himself. He is our nourishment both spiritually and physically, metaphorically and actually. When we participate in the Eucharist, we call to mind his passion, death, and resurrection. We consume him who is the Bread of Life.

Connecting the Responsorial Psalm to the Readings

Our responsorial psalm, "Lord, you will show us the path of life," seems to fit in well with today's gospel in which Jesus joins the disciples on the road to Emmaus. The downcast disciples do not realize that they are on the road leading away from their salvation and the good news proclaimed by the empty tomb. Jesus joins them on the path they have chosen and slowly, through opening up the Scriptures and by sharing bread together, leads them to "abounding joy in [his] presence." After he has vanished from their midst, they immediately set out for Jerusalem on the same seven-mile road they journeyed earlier that day. But this time they are going toward their community with good news of their own to proclaim. This time they are on the path of life.

Psalmist Preparation

How do you experience Jesus as walking beside you and leading you on the path of life?

Prayer

By encountering the stranger on the way,
you heal our grief, O God.
By inviting them to stay with us,
you make the cold night warm and safe.
In the breaking of the bread,
you feed our hearts with hope.
You will show us the path to life. Alleluia!
Abounding joy in your presence. Alleluia!

Gospel (John 10:1-10; L49A)

Jesus said: "Amen, amen, I say to you, whoever does not enter a sheep-fold through the gate but climbs over elsewhere is a thief and a robber. But whoever enters through the gate is the shepherd of the sheep. The gatekeeper opens it for him, and the sheep hear his voice, as the shepherd calls his own sheep by name and leads them out. When he has driven  out all his own, he walks ahead of them, and the sheep follow him, because they recognize his voice. But they will not follow a stranger; they will run away from him, because they do not recognize the voice of strangers." Although Jesus used this figure of speech, the Pharisees did not realize what he was trying to tell them.

So Jesus said again, "Amen, amen, I say to you, I am the gate for the sheep. All who came before me are thieves and robbers, but the sheep did not listen to them. I am the gate. Whoever enters through me will be saved, and will come in and go out and find pasture. A thief comes only to steal and slaughter and destroy; I came so that they might have life and have it more abundantly."

First Reading (Acts 2:14a, 36-41)

Then Peter stood up with the Eleven, raised his voice, and proclaimed: "Let the whole house of Israel know for certain that God has made both Lord and Christ, this Jesus whom you crucified."

Now when they heard this, they were cut to the heart, and they asked Peter and the other apostles, "What are we to do, my brothers?" Peter said to them, "Repent and be baptized, every one of you, in the name of Jesus Christ for the forgiveness of your sins; and you will receive the gift of the Holy Spirit. For the promise is made to you and to your children and to all those far off, whomever the Lord our God will call." He testified with many other arguments, and was exhorting them, "Save yourselves from this corrupt generation." Those who accepted his message were baptized, and about three thousand persons were added that day.

Responsorial Psalm (Ps 23:1-3a, 3b-4, 5, 6)

℟. (1) The Lord is my shepherd; there is nothing I shall want.
or: ℟. Alleluia.

The LORD is my shepherd; I shall not want.
    In verdant pastures he gives me repose;
beside restful waters he leads me;
    he refreshes my soul.

℟. The Lord is my shepherd; there is nothing I shall want.
 or: ℟. Alleluia.

He guides me in right paths
    for his name's sake.
Even though I walk in the dark valley
    I fear no evil; for you are at my side
with your rod and your staff
    that give me courage.

℟. The Lord is my shepherd; there is nothing I shall want.
 or: ℟. Alleluia.

You spread the table before me
    in the sight of my foes;
you anoint my head with oil;
    my cup overflows.

℟. The Lord is my shepherd; there is nothing I shall want.
 or: ℟. Alleluia.

Only goodness and kindness follow me
    all the days of my life;
and I shall dwell in the house of the LORD
    for years to come.

℟. The Lord is my shepherd; there is nothing I shall want.
 or: ℟. Alleluia.

See Appendix, p. 206, for Second Reading

Reflecting on Living the Gospel

We are sheep; Jesus is the gate for the sheepfold. The imagery is simple and ancient. Here there is not "heaven" but instead a place of safety and security from the world with its dangers and threats. Even this place of safety is not entirely secure, as there are some thieves and robbers who would climb the fence, not entering through the gate. Our only "protection" from such dangers is that we would not follow their voice. Let us know the gate through which we enter the sheepfold and not be called away by other voices.

Connecting the Responsorial Psalm to the Readings

The abundant life Jesus offers to his disciples is illustrated beautifully in Psalm 23. With God as our Shepherd there is nothing we lack. Like a gracious host, the Lord sets a table before us and anoints our head with oil. It is no surprise the imagery of sheep and shepherds appears so frequently in the Bible. Shepherds keeping watch over their flock would have been a common sight in the land of Israel. Many of the patriarchs of ancient Israel were sheepherders, including Abraham, Isaac, and Jacob, not to mention King David (to whom this psalm is ascribed) and Moses, who meets God in the burning bush while "tending the flock of his father-in-law Jethro" (Exod 3:1; NABRE).

Psalmist Preparation

Only a shepherd could fully understand the vulnerability of domesticated sheep when there is no one to guide them, or the relationship that can be built up between a shepherd and the flock he tenderly cares for. How do you experience God as a Shepherd?

Prayer

When we fear we do not have enough,
Good Shepherd, guide us.
When we doubt our own worth,
Good Shepherd, encourage us.
When we believe we are alone,
Good Shepherd, call to us.
The Lord is my shepherd. Alleluia!
There is nothing I shall want. Alleluia!

Gospel (John 14:1-12; L52A)

Jesus said to his disciples: "Do not let your hearts be troubled. You have faith in God; have faith also in me. In my Father's house there are many dwelling places. If there were not, would I have told you that I am going to prepare a place for you? And if I go and prepare a place for you, I will come back again and take you to myself, so that where I am you also may be. Where I am going you know the

way." Thomas said to him, "Master, we do not know where you are going; how can we know the way?" Jesus said to him, "I am the way and the truth and the life. No one comes to the Father except through me. If you know me, then you will also know my Father. From now on you do know him and have seen him." Philip said to him, "Master, show us the Father, and that will be enough for us." Jesus said to him, "Have I been with you for so long a time and you still do not know me, Philip? Whoever has seen me has seen the Father. How can you say, 'Show us the Father'? Do you not believe that I am in the Father and the Father is in me? The words that I speak to you I do not speak on my own. The Father who dwells in me is doing his works. Believe me that I am in the Father and the Father is in me, or else, believe because of the works themselves. Amen, amen, I say to you, whoever believes in me will do the works that I do, and will do greater ones than these, because I am going to the Father."

First Reading (Acts 6:1-7)

As the number of disciples continued to grow, the Hellenists complained against the Hebrews because their widows were being neglected in the daily distribution. So the Twelve called together the community of the disciples and said, "It is not right for us to neglect the word of God to serve at table. Brothers, select from among you seven reputable men, filled with the Spirit and wisdom, whom we shall appoint to this task, whereas we shall devote ourselves to prayer and to the ministry of the word." The proposal was acceptable to the whole community, so they chose Stephen, a man filled with faith and the Holy Spirit, also Philip,

Prochorus, Nicanor, Timon, Parmenas, and Nicholas of Antioch, a convert to Judaism. They presented these men to the apostles who prayed and laid hands on them. The word of God continued to spread, and the number of the disciples in Jerusalem increased greatly; even a large group of priests were becoming obedient to the faith.

Responsorial Psalm (Ps 33:1-2, 4-5, 18-19)

℟. (22) Lord, let your mercy be on us, as we place our trust in you.
or: ℟. Alleluia.

Exult, you just, in the LORD;
  praise from the upright is fitting.
Give thanks to the LORD on the harp;
  with the ten-stringed lyre chant his praises.

℟. Lord, let your mercy be on us, as we place our trust in you.
or: ℟. Alleluia.

Upright is the word of the LORD,
  and all his works are trustworthy.
He loves justice and right;
  of the kindness of the LORD the earth is full.

℟. Lord, let your mercy be on us, as we place our trust in you.
or: ℟. Alleluia.

See, the eyes of the LORD are upon those who fear him,
  upon those who hope for his kindness,
to deliver them from death
  and preserve them in spite of famine.

℟. Lord, let your mercy be on us, as we place our trust in you.
or: ℟. Alleluia.

See Appendix, p. 206, for Second Reading

Reflecting on Living the Gospel

The relationship between Jesus and the Father cannot be reduced to a mathematical formula; it is not an engineering problem. It is a dynamic rather than static relationship. It is not reducible to quantifiable precision, as we might expect in a chemistry lab. Ultimately, we are dealing with imagery, metaphor, and analogy for the divine, which cannot be boxed up, packaged, and distributed in discrete packets of knowledge. The gospel reading invites us to enter into this dynamic relationship between the Father and the Son, God and the Word. Once engaged, this dynamic relationship never ends, but only continues, often deepens, and typically challenges.

Connecting the Responsorial Psalm to the Readings

Our responsorial psalm prays, "Lord, let your mercy be on us, as we place our trust in you." In the gospel the disciples are called to place all of their trust in Jesus as their way to God, their pillar of truth, and their entry into abundant and everlasting life. This was a difficult thing to ask of them, especially on the night before Jesus' crucifixion. The words he spoke of where he was going and his relationship to the Father still baffled and confused most of the disciples. And yet, even after their desertion of him during his passion and death, Jesus spends the time between his resurrection and ascension searching out and restoring those who had faltered. In his love and mercy, Jesus—our way, truth, and life— proves himself eminently trustworthy.

Psalmist Preparation

The psalmist sings, "Upright is the word of the Lord, / and all his works are trustworthy." What events and experiences in your life have led you to trust in the Lord?

Prayer

Upright is your word, O God,
for you are the way, the truth, and the life.
All your works are trustworthy,
for you are the way, the truth, and the life.
Help us believe and follow you,
for you are the way, the truth, and the life.
Exult, you just, in the Lord. Alleluia!
Give thanks to the Lord. Alleluia!

Gospel (John 14:15-21; L55A)

Jesus said to his disciples: "If you love me, you will keep my commandments. And I will ask the Father, and he will give you another Advocate to be with you always, the Spirit of truth, whom the world cannot accept, because it neither sees nor knows him. But you know him, because he remains with you, and will be in you. I will not leave you orphans; I will come to you. In a little while the world will no longer see me, but you will see me, because I live and you will live. On that day you will realize that I am in my Father and you are in me and I in you. Whoever has my commandments and observes them is the one who loves me. And whoever loves me will be loved by my Father, and I will love him and reveal myself to him."

First Reading (Acts 8:5-8, 14-17)

Philip went down to the city of Samaria and proclaimed the Christ to them. With one accord, the crowds paid attention to what was said by Philip when they heard it and saw the signs he was doing. For unclean spirits, crying out in a loud voice, came out of many possessed people, and many paralyzed or crippled people were cured. There was great joy in that city.

Now when the apostles in Jerusalem heard that Samaria had accepted the word of God, they sent them Peter and John, who went down and prayed for them, that they might receive the Holy Spirit, for it had not yet fallen upon any of them; they had only been baptized in the name of the Lord Jesus. Then they laid hands on them and they received the Holy Spirit.

Responsorial Psalm (Ps 66:1-3, 4-5, 6-7, 16, 20)

℞. (1) Let all the earth cry out to God with joy. *or:* ℞. Alleluia.

Shout joyfully to God, all the earth,
    sing praise to the glory of his name;
    proclaim his glorious praise.
Say to God, "How tremendous are your deeds!"

℞. Let all the earth cry out to God with joy. *or:* ℞. Alleluia.

"Let all on earth worship and sing praise to you,
    sing praise to your name!"
Come and see the works of God,
    his tremendous deeds among the children of Adam.

℞. Let all the earth cry out to God with joy. *or:* ℞. Alleluia.

He has changed the sea into dry land;
    through the river they passed on foot;
    therefore let us rejoice in him.
He rules by his might forever.

℞. Let all the earth cry out to God with joy. *or:* ℞. Alleluia.

Hear now, all you who fear God, while I declare
    what he has done for me.
Blessed be God who refused me not
    my prayer or his kindness!

℞. Let all the earth cry out to God with joy. *or:* ℞. Alleluia.

See Appendix, p. 207, for Second Reading

Reflecting on Living the Gospel

As Christians we seek to follow the example of Christ, who poured himself out in love. Love knows no limits and there is not a point when we
say "enough." Love sees the other as another self, so that the needs of
the other are as important as our own. When modern communication
has made the world a global village, the needs of our neighbors can
seem overwhelming. Where do we stop? Yet, we are called to move beyond ourselves as Jesus did and to place our lives in service of the other,
in imitation of him. Then we may merit the name "disciple," when we are
known by our love.

Connecting the Responsorial Psalm to the Readings

Our psalm for today is one of joy and praise, an apt response to the hap-
penings in the first reading in which Philip proclaims Christ to the
people of Samaria and performs signs of God's power by healing the
paralyzed, crippled, and possessed. The psalmist calls for us to "[c]ome
and see the works of God, / his tremendous deeds among the children of
Adam." From the central event in the Old Testament (mentioned in

today's psalm) when the Israelites passed through the sea "on foot" to escape slavery in Egypt, we could say that God's greatest works are all oriented to freedom: freedom from slavery, freedom from brokenness in mind, body, or spirit, and freedom from sin. Freedom is necessary for prayer. True praise and worship cannot be coerced or demanded.

Psalmist Preparation

As you lead today's psalm calling for "all the earth to cry out to God with joy," consider where you might need God's freeing action in your life so as to praise him even more fully.

Prayer

If we love you, Lord, our God,
we will keep your commandments.
If we love you, Lord, our God,
we will never be orphaned.
May Christ the Lord be Lord in our hearts,
and we will keep your commandments.
Let all the earth cry out with joy. Alleluia!
Sing praise to the glory of God's name. Alleluia!

MAY 21 OR 24, 2020

Gospel (Matt 28:16-20; L58A)

The eleven disciples went to Galilee, to the mountain to which Jesus had ordered them. When they saw him, they worshiped, but they doubted. Then Jesus approached and said to them, "All power in heaven and on earth has been given to me. Go, therefore, and make disciples of all nations, baptizing them in the name of the Father, and of the Son, and of the Holy Spirit, teaching them to observe all that I have commanded you. And behold, I am with you always, until the end of the age."

First Reading (Acts 1:1-11)

In the first book, Theophilus, I dealt with all that Jesus did and taught until the day he was taken up, after giving instructions through the Holy Spirit to the apostles whom he had chosen. He presented himself alive to them by many proofs after he had suffered, appearing to them during forty days and speaking about the kingdom of God. While meeting with them, he enjoined them not to depart from Jerusalem, but to wait for "the promise of the Father about which you have heard me speak; for John baptized with water, but in a few days you will be baptized with the Holy Spirit."

When they had gathered together they asked him, "Lord, are you at this time going to restore the kingdom to Israel?" He answered them, "It is not for you to know the times or seasons that the Father has established by his own authority. But you will receive power when the Holy Spirit comes upon you, and you will be my witnesses in Jerusalem, throughout Judea and Samaria, and to the ends of the earth." When he had said this, as they were looking on, he was lifted up, and a cloud took him from their sight. While they were looking intently at the sky as he was going, suddenly two men dressed in white garments stood beside them. They said, "Men of Galilee, why are you standing there looking at the sky? This Jesus who has been taken up from you into heaven will return in the same way as you have seen him going into heaven."

Responsorial Psalm (Ps 47:2-3, 6-7, 8-9)

℟. (6) God mounts his throne to shouts of joy: a blare of trumpets for the Lord. *or:* ℟. Alleluia.

All you peoples, clap your hands,
    shout to God with cries of gladness,
for the LORD, the Most High, the awesome,
    is the great king over all the earth.

℟. God mounts his throne to shouts of joy: a blare of trumpets for the Lord. *or:* ℟. Alleluia.

God mounts his throne amid shouts of joy;
    the LORD, amid trumpet blasts.
Sing praise to God, sing praise;
    sing praise to our king, sing praise.

℟. God mounts his throne to shouts of joy: a blare of trumpets for the Lord. *or:* ℟. Alleluia.

For king of all the earth is God;
    sing hymns of praise.
God reigns over the nations,
    God sits upon his holy throne.

℟. God mounts his throne to shouts of joy: a blare of trumpets for the Lord. *or:* ℟. Alleluia.

See Appendix, p. 207, for Second Reading

Reflecting on Living the Gospel

The ascension is depicted so graphically in Acts that many of us read Matthew's story with Acts in the background. But the story of the ascension is not so much about Jesus magically rising into the air and being taken away by clouds, as it is about the last time he was seen by his disciples. Theologically, the important aspect is what he says, not how he leaves. In the Gospel of Matthew, he commissions the disciples to evangelize, to tell the good news, making disciples on their way by baptizing. We, like the disciples, are sent on mission—to live the gospel values.

Connecting the Responsorial Psalm to the Readings

Today's psalm is one of the most triumphant in the whole book of
Psalms. It paints a picture we can clearly see in our minds as well as
hear, with the sounds of trumpets blaring and the joyful shouts of the
thronging crowds. Jesus' words to the disciples in Matthew's gospel are
also triumphant. He tells them, "All power in heaven and on earth has
been given to me." With the power he has been given, Jesus commissions
the disciples to go out to all the nations and baptize "in the name of the
Father, / and of the Son, and of the Holy Spirit." It is fitting that our
psalm ends with the affirmation "[f]or king of all the earth is God . . .
God reigns over all the nations."

Psalmist Preparation

In the second verse of today's psalm, we are called to "[s]ing praise to
God, sing praise; / sing praise to our king, sing praise." In your daily life,
how do you offer praise to God the King?

Prayer

Call us to go and make disciples, Lord,
for you are with us always;
to baptize them in your holy name,
for you are with us always;
and teach them to follow your way of love,
for you are with us always.
Sing praise to God, sing praise. Alleluia!
All people of God, sing hymns of praise. Alleluia!

Gospel (John 17:1-11a; L59A)

Jesus raised his eyes to heaven and said,
"Father, the hour has come. Give glory to
your son, so that your son may glorify you,
just as you gave him authority over all
people, so that your son may give eternal
life to all you gave him. Now this is eternal
life, that they should know you, the only
true God, and the one whom you sent,
Jesus Christ. I glorified you on earth by ac-
complishing the work that you gave me to
do. Now glorify me, Father, with you, with
the glory that I had with you before the
world began.

"I revealed your name to those whom
you gave me out of the world. They be-
longed to you, and you gave them to me,
and they have kept your word. Now they
know that everything you gave me is from you, because the words you
gave to me I have given to them, and they accepted them and truly
understood that I came from you, and they have believed that you sent
me. I pray for them. I do not pray for the world but for the ones you have
given me, because they are yours, and everything of mine is yours and
everything of yours is mine, and I have been glorified in them. And now
I will no longer be in the world, but they are in the world, while I am
coming to you."

First Reading (Acts 1:12-14)

After Jesus had been taken up to heaven the apostles returned to Jerusalem from the mount called Olivet, which is near Jerusalem, a sabbath
day's journey away.

When they entered the city they went to the upper room where they
were staying, Peter and John and James and Andrew, Philip and Thomas,
Bartholomew and Matthew, James son of Alphaeus, Simon the Zealot,
and Judas son of James. All these devoted themselves with one accord to
prayer, together with some women, and Mary the mother of Jesus, and
his brothers.

Responsorial Psalm (Ps 27:1, 4, 7-8)

℟. (13) I believe that I shall see the good things of the Lord in the land of the living. *or:* ℟. Alleluia.

The LORD is my light and my salvation;
  whom should I fear?
The LORD is my life's refuge;
  of whom should I be afraid?

℟. I believe that I shall see the good things of the Lord in the land of the living. *or:* ℟. Alleluia.

One thing I ask of the LORD;
  this I seek:
to dwell in the house of the LORD
  all the days of my life,
that I may gaze on the loveliness of the LORD
  and contemplate his temple.

℟. I believe that I shall see the good things of the Lord in the land of the living. *or:* ℟. Alleluia.

Hear, O LORD, the sound of my call;
  have pity on me, and answer me.
Of you my heart speaks; you my glance seeks.

℟. I believe that I shall see the good things of the Lord in the land of the living. *or:* ℟. Alleluia.

See Appendix, p. 207, for Second Reading

Reflecting on Living the Gospel

The night before he died, Jesus prayed for us and for all those who were chosen by God. Rather than make us smug, this knowledge should humble us and cause us to emulate him who came to serve rather than be served. We live in the world but are not of the world. It is only a temporary home for us. A bright future awaits where love reigns and glory is resplendent. For Jesus in the Gospel of John, the crucifixion is the lifting up, the exaltation of the Son of God. With eyes of faith, let us see anew and reorient our lives.

Connecting the Responsorial Psalm to the Readings

While today's first reading and gospel lift up moments of prayer, the second reading from the first letter of St. Peter centers on a different theme, rejoicing in suffering. We know that the apostles who gather in the Upper Room to await the gift of the Holy Spirit will live boldly in witness to Christ. Most of their lives will end in violent death, and yet, even as they see their closest companions martyred, the apostles are not deterred from proclaiming Jesus to all they meet. We might ask, where did their tenacity in the face of death arise from? Our psalm response suggests an answer—unshakeable hope and trust in the God of life: "I believe that I shall see the good things of the Lord in the land of the living."

Psalmist Preparation

As you prepare to lead the assembly in song and prayer, consider this question: What is the hope that you cling to even in the midst of suffering or fear?

Prayer

As he prepared to die on the cross,
Jesus prayed for us.
Though the hour of his death had come,
Jesus prayed for us.
Teach us to pray with one accord,
as Jesus prayed for us.
The Lord is my light and my salvation. Alleluia!
The Lord is my life's refuge. Alleluia!

Gospel (John 20:19-23; L63A)

On the evening of that first day of the week, when the doors were locked, where the disciples were, for fear of the Jews, Jesus came and stood in their midst and said to them, "Peace be with you." When he had said this, he showed them his hands and his side. The disciples rejoiced when they saw the Lord. Jesus said to them again, "Peace be with you. As the Father has sent me, so I send you." And when he had said this, he breathed on them and said to them, "Receive the Holy Spirit. Whose sins you forgive are forgiven them, and whose sins you retain are retained."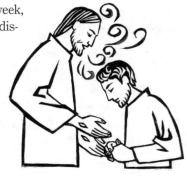

First Reading (Acts 2:1-11)

When the time for Pentecost was fulfilled, they were all in one place together. And suddenly there came from the sky a noise like a strong driving wind, and it filled the entire house in which they were. Then there appeared to them tongues as of fire, which parted and came to rest on each one of them. And they were all filled with the Holy Spirit and began to speak in different tongues, as the Spirit enabled them to proclaim.

Now there were devout Jews from every nation under heaven staying in Jerusalem. At this sound, they gathered in a large crowd, but they were confused because each one heard them speaking in his own language. They were astounded, and in amazement they asked, "Are not all these people who are speaking Galileans? Then how does each of us hear them in his native language? We are Parthians, Medes, and Elamites, inhabitants of Mesopotamia, Judea and Cappadocia, Pontus and Asia, Phrygia and Pamphylia, Egypt and the districts of Libya near Cyrene, as well as travelers from Rome, both Jews and converts to Judaism, Cretans and Arabs, yet we hear them speaking in our own tongues of the mighty acts of God."

Responsorial Psalm (Ps 104:1, 24, 29-30, 31, 34)

R︎. (cf. 30) Lord, send out your Spirit, and renew the face of the earth.
or: R︎. Alleluia.

Bless the LORD, O my soul!
  O LORD, my God, you are great indeed!
How manifold are your works, O LORD!
  The earth is full of your creatures.

R︎. Lord, send out your Spirit, and renew the face of the earth.
or: R︎. Alleluia.

If you take away their breath, they perish
  and return to their dust.
When you send forth your spirit, they are created,
  and you renew the face of the earth.

R︎. Lord, send out your Spirit, and renew the face of the earth.
or: R︎. Alleluia.

May the glory of the LORD endure forever;
  may the LORD be glad in his works!
Pleasing to him be my theme;
  I will be glad in the LORD.

R︎. Lord, send out your Spirit, and renew the face of the earth.
or: R︎. Alleluia.

See Appendix, p. 207, for Second Reading

Reflecting on Living the Gospel
What would it have been like to have seen the risen Jesus and to have heard him say, "Peace be with you" before handing on the Holy Spirit? Yet, for those of us in the twenty-first century, we experience that same Holy Spirit. When we were baptized, we were given the gift of the Spirit, and then we were sealed by that same spirit in confirmation. The Holy Spirit lives in our parishes, families, friends, and relationships. After he rose from the dead, Jesus gave his Holy Spirit to be with us. In our daily lives, let us allow ourselves to be guided by the Spirit of Christ, whose disciples we are.

Connecting the Responsorial Psalm to the Readings

Not only does the Spirit bless humans, it sustains and renews all of creation, as our psalm announces. From the first two verses of Genesis we hear how when "God created the heavens and the earth . . . the earth was formless and empty, darkness was over the surface of the deep, and the Spirit of God was hovering over the waters" (1:1-2; NIV). Just as God's Spirit created order in the cosmos and on our planet at the time of creation, it continues to bring beauty from chaos. The psalmist proclaims, "When you send forth your spirit, they are created, / and you renew the face of the earth."

Psalmist Preparation

On the feast of Pentecost we ask in a particular way for the Holy Spirit to be poured out upon us and upon all of creation. Where are you most in need of the Spirit's renewing presence in your life?

Prayer

Come, Spirit, come:
from your celestial home!
Come, Spirit, come:
the Source of all good!
Come, Spirit, come:
most blessed Light divine!
Fill the hearts of your faithful. Alleluia!
And kindle in them the fire of your love. Alleluia!

Gospel (John 3:16-18; L164A)

God so loved the world that he gave his only Son, so that everyone who believes in him might not perish but might have eternal life. For God did not send his Son into the world to condemn the world, but that the world might be saved through him. Whoever believes in him will not be condemned, but whoever does not believe has already been condemned, because he has not believed in the name of the only Son of God.

First Reading (Exod 34:4b-6, 8-9)

Early in the morning Moses went up Mount Sinai as the LORD had commanded him, taking along the two stone tablets.

Having come down in a cloud, the LORD stood with Moses there and proclaimed his name, "LORD." Thus the LORD passed before him and cried out, "The LORD, the LORD, a merciful and gracious God, slow to anger and rich in kindness and fidelity." Moses at once bowed down to the ground in worship. Then he said, "If I find favor with you, O LORD, do come along in our company. This is indeed a stiff-necked people; yet pardon our wickedness and sins, and receive us as your own."

Responsorial Psalm (Dan 3:52, 53, 54, 55)

℟. (52b) Glory and praise for ever!

Blessed are you, O Lord, the God of our fathers,
    praiseworthy and exalted above all forever;
and blessed is your holy and glorious name,
    praiseworthy and exalted above all for all ages.

℟. Glory and praise for ever!

Blessed are you in the temple of your holy glory,
    praiseworthy and glorious above all forever.

℟. Glory and praise for ever!

Blessed are you on the throne of your kingdom,
    praiseworthy and exalted above all forever.

℟. Glory and praise for ever!

Blessed are you who look into the depths
　　from your throne upon the cherubim,
　　praiseworthy and exalted above all forever.

℟. Glory and praise for ever!

See Appendix, p. 208, for Second Reading

Reflecting on Living the Gospel

On this, the feast of the Most Holy Trinity, we have one of the shortest
gospel readings of the year. The passage is only three verses and it is
proclaimed at the eucharistic liturgy often in less than a minute, no more
than two. The opening line of this gospel reading will be familiar to
many as it may be used frequently to sum up Christian theology: "God so
loved the world that he gave his only Son." This is a model for action motivated by love. We are to be givers, disciples of the Son of God who was
given to the world.

Connecting the Responsorial Psalm to the Readings

Today's responsorial psalm is not from the book of Psalms at all but
from the book of Daniel. It is taken from the canticle of the three youths,
cast into the fiery furnace by King Nebuchadnezzar who had demanded
that they fall down in worship before a golden statue. Although the king
has the fire stoked to seven times its usual heat (Dan 3:19), the young
men are unharmed, for "the angel of the Lord went down . . . [and]
drove the fiery flames out of the furnace" (Dan 3:49; NABRE). In response, the three young men sing to the glory of God the first four
verses of which we sing today in our psalm. On this feast of the Most
Holy Trinity we pronounce that our God, Father, Son, and Holy Spirit, is
"praiseworthy and exalted above all for all forever."

Psalmist Preparation

In your own life of faith, what helps you give glory and praise to our
triune God in the midst of struggle and hardship?

Prayer

Out of so great a love, Father, you sent your Son to save us.
Through your Holy Spirit, unite us in love
that we may share in your eternal life.
Glory to the Father, the Son, and the Holy Spirit:
Glory and praise forever! Amen.

Gospel (John 6:51-58; L167A)

Jesus said to the Jewish crowds: "I am the living bread that came down from heaven; whoever eats this bread will live forever; and the bread that I will give is my flesh for the life of the world."

The Jews quarreled among themselves, saying, "How can this man give us his flesh to eat?" Jesus said to them, "Amen, amen, I say to you, unless you eat the flesh of the Son of Man and drink his blood, you do not have life within you. Whoever eats my flesh and drinks my blood has eternal life, and I will raise him on the last day. For my flesh is true food, and my blood is true drink. Whoever eats my flesh and drinks my blood remains in me and I in him. Just as the living Father sent me and I have life because of the Father, so also the one who feeds on me will have life because of me. This is the bread that came down from heaven. Unlike your ancestors who ate and still died, whoever eats this bread will live forever."

First Reading (Deut 8:2-3, 14b-16a)

Moses said to the people: "Remember how for forty years now the LORD, your God, has directed all your journeying in the desert, so as to test you by affliction and find out whether or not it was your intention to keep his commandments. He therefore let you be afflicted with hunger, and then fed you with manna, a food unknown to you and your fathers, in order to show you that not by bread alone does one live, but by every word that comes forth from the mouth of the LORD.

"Do not forget the LORD, your God, who brought you out of the land of Egypt, that place of slavery; who guided you through the vast and terrible desert with its saraph serpents and scorpions, its parched and waterless ground; who brought forth water for you from the flinty rock and fed you in the desert with manna, a food unknown to your fathers."

Responsorial Psalm (Ps 147:12-13, 14-15, 19-20)

R̸. (12) Praise the Lord, Jerusalem. *or:* R̸. Alleluia.

Glorify the LORD, O Jerusalem;
    praise your God, O Zion.
For he has strengthened the bars of your gates;
    he has blessed your children within you.

R̸. Praise the Lord, Jerusalem. *or:* R̸. Alleluia.

He has granted peace in your borders;
    with the best of wheat he fills you.
He sends forth his command to the earth;
    swiftly runs his word!

R̸. Praise the Lord, Jerusalem. *or:* R̸. Alleluia.

He has proclaimed his word to Jacob,
    his statutes and his ordinances to Israel.
He has not done thus for any other nation;
    his ordinances he has not made known to them. Alleluia.

R̸. Praise the Lord, Jerusalem. *or:* R̸. Alleluia.

See Appendix, p. 208, for Second Reading

Reflecting on Living the Gospel

The gospel reading for the feast of Corpus Christi is not from the Last
Supper as we might expect. Instead, the reading is from part of the
"bread of life discourse" of the Gospel of John. The eucharistic theology
is upfront and paramount. Jesus proclaims that he is the living bread
come down from heaven. And so that his listeners might not misunder-
stand, he states clearly that this is true food and true drink. The imagery
is so stark that many stumble over this teaching. Still Jesus maintains
that those who consume this bread will live forever.

Connecting the Responsorial Psalm to the Readings

Psalm 147 illustrates the abundant blessings the God of Israel showers
upon his people. They dwell secure because "he has strengthened the
bars of [Jerusalem's] gates" and "granted peace within [Jerusalem's] borders." They are sustained "with the best of wheat" and shepherded by
the very "statutes" and "ordinances" of the Lord, which "he has not

made known to [other nations]." On this feast of Corpus Christi, we also celebrate the care God has bestowed upon us by feeding us at the table of the Lord and sustaining us with his Word and commandments. In these abundant blessings we are also called to be a blessing to others. In the first letter to the Corinthians, St. Paul asks, "The cup of blessing that we bless, / is it not a participation in the blood of Christ? / The bread that we break, / is it not a participation in the body of Christ?" We know that Jesus' blood was poured out and his body broken that it might redeem the world.

Psalmist Preparation

How are you called to be poured out, blessed, broken, and shared for the life of the world as a participant in the Body and Blood of Christ?

Prayer

We praise you, Lord, for you have blessed us
with a shelter strong and peaceful lives.
Unite us in the one cup and the one bread we share in Christ.
Blood is poured and flesh is broken.
From our hearts let praises sing. Amen.

Gospel (Matt 10:26-33; L94A)

Jesus said to the Twelve: "Fear no one. Nothing is concealed that will not be revealed, nor secret that will not be known. What I say to you in the darkness, speak in the light; what you hear whispered, proclaim on the housetops. And do not be afraid of those who kill the body but cannot kill the soul; rather, be afraid of the one who can destroy both soul and body in Gehenna. Are not two sparrows sold for a small coin? Yet not one of them falls to the ground without your Father's knowledge. Even all the hairs of your head are counted. So do not be  afraid; you are worth more than many sparrows. Everyone who acknowledges me before others I will acknowledge before my heavenly Father. But whoever denies me before others, I will deny before my heavenly Father."

First Reading (Jer 20:10-13)

Jeremiah said:

"I hear the whisperings of many:
'Terror on every side!
Denounce! Let us denounce him!'
All those who were my friends
are on the watch for any misstep of mine.
'Perhaps he will be trapped; then we can prevail,
and take our vengeance on him.'
But the LORD is with me, like a mighty champion:
my persecutors will stumble, they will not triumph.
In their failure they will be put to utter shame,
to lasting, unforgettable confusion.
O LORD of hosts, you who test the just,
who probe mind and heart,
let me witness the vengeance you take on them,
for to you I have entrusted my cause.

Sing to the LORD,
    praise the LORD,
for he has rescued the life of the poor
    from the power of the wicked!"

Responsorial Psalm (Ps 69:8-10, 14, 17, 33-35)

R̸. (14c) Lord, in your great love, answer me.

For your sake I bear insult,
    and shame covers my face.
I have become an outcast to my brothers,
    a stranger to my children,
because zeal for your house consumes me,
    and the insults of those who blaspheme you fall upon me.

R̸. Lord, in your great love, answer me.

I pray to you, O LORD,
    for the time of your favor, O God!
In your great kindness answer me
    with your constant help.
Answer me, O LORD, for bounteous is your kindness;
    in your great mercy turn toward me.

R̸. Lord, in your great love, answer me.

"See, you lowly ones, and be glad;
    you who seek God, may your hearts revive!
For the LORD hears the poor,
    and his own who are in bonds he spurns not.
Let the heavens and the earth praise him,
    the seas and whatever moves in them!"

R̸. Lord, in your great love, answer me.

Second Reading (Rom 5:12-15)

Reflecting on Living the Gospel

In the reading we hear today, Jesus says to his disciples three times some variation of "fear not" or "do not be afraid." The disciples (and that includes us) are to be fearless. The basis of this fearlessness is the Father, who knows all—even the most seemingly insignificant things that we do not know (e.g., the hairs on our head). The Father even knows each and every sparrow. We, as human beings, are individually worth more than two sparrows (which themselves were worth only a small coin in antiquity). So the disciples can rest assured: they can be fearless in facing the world, as they are worth a great deal in the sight of God.

Connecting the Responsorial Psalm to the Readings

The psalmist sings, "[Z]eal for your house consumes me." This zeal leads to shame and insults, and even to being cast out from family and friends. As with the first reading from Jeremiah, even though this psalm begins with despair it ends in hope, for despite current difficulties, "the Lord hears the poor, / and his own who are in bonds he spurns not." For this reason, the psalmist will continue to praise the Lord. It is the same hope and joy that the apostles are called on to have in the gospel. Though they might face persecution, they are protected unto eternal life by the God of creation. They need not fear.

Psalmist Preparation

Has there been a time in your life when you prayed with the conviction and desperation of today's psalm asking, "Lord, in your great love, answer me"? What did this time teach you about faith?

Prayer

O God, you have rescued the life of the poor
from the power of the wicked.
May we never be afraid to proclaim your Gospel.
Let the heavens and the earth praise God
who hears and answers those in need. Amen.

Gospel (Matt 10:37-42; L97A)

Jesus said to his apostles: "Whoever loves father or mother more than me is not worthy of me, and whoever loves son or daughter more than me is not worthy of me; and whoever does not take up his cross and follow after me is not worthy of me. Whoever finds his life will lose it, and whoever loses his life for my sake will find it. Whoever receives you receives me, and whoever receives me receives the one who sent me. Whoever receives a prophet because he is a prophet will receive a prophet's reward, and whoever receives a righteous man because he is a righteous man will receive a righteous man's reward. And whoever gives only a cup of cold water to one of these little ones to drink because the little one is a disciple—amen, I say to you, he will surely not lose his reward."

First Reading (2 Kgs 4:8-11, 14-16a)

One day Elisha came to Shunem, where there was a woman of influence, who urged him to dine with her. Afterward, whenever he passed by, he used to stop there to dine. So she said to her husband, "I know that Elisha is a holy man of God. Since he visits us often, let us arrange a little room on the roof and furnish it for him with a bed, table, chair, and lamp, so that when he comes to us he can stay there." Sometime later Elisha arrived and stayed in the room overnight.

Later Elisha asked, "Can something be done for her?" His servant Gehazi answered, "Yes! She has no son, and her husband is getting on in years." Elisha said, "Call her." When the woman had been called and stood at the door, Elisha promised, "This time next year you will be fondling a baby son."

Responsorial Psalm (Ps 89:2-3, 16-17, 18-19)

R℣. (2a) For ever I will sing the goodness of the Lord.

The promises of the Lord I will sing forever,
    through all generations my mouth shall proclaim your faithfulness.
For you have said, "My kindness is established forever";
    in heaven you have confirmed your faithfulness.

R℣. For ever I will sing the goodness of the Lord.

Blessed the people who know the joyful shout;
   in the light of your countenance, O LORD, they walk.
At your name they rejoice all the day,
   and through your justice they are exalted.

R℣. For ever I will sing the goodness of the Lord.

You are the splendor of their strength,
   and by your favor our horn is exalted.
For to the LORD belongs our shield,
   and to the Holy One of Israel, our king.

R℣. For ever I will sing the goodness of the Lord.

Second Reading (Rom 6:3-4, 8-11)

Reflecting on Living the Gospel
The paschal mystery is a paradox par excellence. Suffering and death
lead to new life and resurrection. There can be no resurrection without
death. There is no new life without casting aside the old. When we listen
to the words of Jesus in today's gospel, we might be especially attuned to
the notion of paradox expressed in the saying about finding our lives—
for to find our lives, we must lose them. We surrender ourselves to the
will of God and thereby find ultimate meaning and purpose. As Augus-
tine said, "[O]ur hearts are restless until they rest in you Lord."

Connecting the Responsorial Psalm to the Readings
Today's psalm of joy and praise seems to be a fitting response from the
childless woman who is promised a son. At that time, a woman who
became widowed would rely on her sons for support. If a woman had
no sons, she would be at the mercy of the community to provide for
her. The woman of Shunem was in danger of this fate since "her husband was getting on in years." When Elisha prophesies that she will
have a son, this not only meant that she would enjoy the blessings of
children but also that she would be protected from destitution when her
husband died.

Psalmist Preparation

Today's psalm is a litany to God's goodness. In the Lord is found light, kindness, justice, strength, and protection. What would be your litany (list) of the blessings of the Lord in your life?

Prayer

Great is the reward you give, O God, to disciples who care for those in need.

Help us to give of our lives and take up our cross
that we may worthily follow your Son.

Forever I will sing the goodness of the Lord.

Through all generations my mouth shall sing God's praise. Amen.

Gospel (Matt 11:25-30; L100A)

At that time Jesus exclaimed: "I give praise to you, Father, Lord of heaven and earth, for although you have hidden these things from the wise and the learned you have revealed them to little ones. Yes, Father, such has been your gracious will. All things have been handed over to me by my Father. No one knows the Son except the Father, and no one knows the Father except the Son and anyone to whom the Son wishes to reveal him.

"Come to me, all you who labor and are burdened, and I will give you rest. Take my yoke upon you and learn from me, for I am meek and humble of heart; and you will find rest for yourselves. For my yoke is easy, and my burden light."

First Reading (Zech 9:9-10)

Thus says the LORD:
   Rejoice heartily, O daughter Zion,
      shout for joy, O daughter Jerusalem!
   See, your king shall come to you;
      a just savior is he,
   meek, and riding on an ass,
      on a colt, the foal of an ass.
   He shall banish the chariot from Ephraim,
      and the horse from Jerusalem;
   the warrior's bow shall be banished,
      and he shall proclaim peace to the nations.
   His dominion shall be from sea to sea,
      and from the River to the ends of the earth.

Responsorial Psalm (Ps 145:1-2, 8-9, 10-11, 13-14)

R℣. (cf. 1) I will praise your name for ever, my king and my God.
or: R℣. Alleluia.

I will extol you, O my God and King,
    and I will bless your name forever and ever.
Every day will I bless you,
    and I will praise your name forever and ever.

R℣. I will praise your name for ever, my king and my God. *or:* R℣. Alleluia.

The LORD is gracious and merciful,
    slow to anger and of great kindness.
The LORD is good to all
    and compassionate toward all his works.

R℣. I will praise your name for ever, my king and my God. *or:* R℣. Alleluia.

Let all your works give you thanks, O LORD,
    and let your faithful ones bless you.
Let them discourse of the glory of your kingdom
    and speak of your might.

R℣. I will praise your name for ever, my king and my God. *or:* R℣. Alleluia.

The LORD is faithful in all his words
    and holy in all his works.
The LORD lifts up all who are falling
    and raises up all who are bowed down.

R℣. I will praise your name for ever, my king and my God. *or:* R℣. Alleluia.

Second Reading (Rom 8:9, 11-13)

Reflecting on Living the Gospel

Bearing a yoke does not seem to be an enjoyable experience. But Jesus gives us this image in today's gospel reading and nearly subverts it. The yoke of Jesus, the one who is meek and humble of heart, is itself easy; the burden is light. In today's gospel, we learn that when we are true disciples of Christ, we conform to the person himself. So conformed, we find any apparent burden not to be a burden at all. We need only act as he would in the world, as another Christ to serve the needs of those around us.

Connecting the Responsorial Psalm to the Readings

Today's psalm is one of praise to God, our king. Rather than lauding God's power and strength, the psalmist highlights the grace and mercy of the Lord who is "slow to anger and of great kindness" and "compassionate toward all his works." Within God, the Father, Son, and Holy Spirit, we find the "Lord of heaven and earth" whose concern is for the humble and the lowly.

Psalmist Preparation

To honor and praise God well, we must hold both images of the Lord in our mind: the one who reigns over heaven and earth in glory and the one who came to dwell among the meek and the lowly and to identify himself among them. How do you balance these two truths in your prayer and life of discipleship?

Prayer

Blessed are you, Father, Lord of heaven and earth;
you have revealed to little ones the mysteries of the kingdom.
Bind us to your humble, gentle yoke.
The Lord lifts up all who are falling
and raises up all who are bowed down. Amen.

Gospel (Matt 13:1-23 [or Matt 13:1-9]; L103A)

On that day, Jesus went out of the house and sat down by the sea. Such large crowds gathered around him that he got into a boat and sat down, and the whole crowd stood along the shore. And he spoke to them at length in parables, saying: "A sower went out to sow. And as he sowed, some seed fell on the path, and birds came and ate it up. Some fell on rocky ground, where it had little soil. It sprang up at once because the soil was not deep, and when the sun rose it was scorched, and it withered for lack of roots. Some seed fell among thorns, and the thorns grew up and choked it. But some seed fell on rich soil, and produced fruit, a hundred or sixty or thirtyfold. Whoever has ears ought to hear."

The disciples approached him and said, "Why do you speak to them in parables?" He said to them in reply, "Because knowledge of the mysteries of the kingdom of heaven has been granted to you, but to them it has not been granted. To anyone who has, more will be given and he will grow rich; from anyone who has not, even what he has will be taken away. This is why I speak to them in parables, because

they look but do not see and hear but do not listen or understand.
Isaiah's prophecy is fulfilled in them, which says:
You shall indeed hear but not understand,
*   you shall indeed look but never see.*
Gross is the heart of this people,
*   they will hardly hear with their ears,*
*   they have closed their eyes,*
*   lest they see with their eyes*
*   and hear with their ears*
and understand with their hearts and be converted,
*   and I heal them.*

"But blessed are your eyes, because they see, and your ears, because they hear. Amen, I say to you, many prophets and righteous people longed to see what you see but did not see it, and to hear what you hear but did not hear it.

"Hear then the parable of the sower. The seed sown on the path is the one who hears the word of the kingdom without understanding it, and the evil one comes and steals away what was sown in his heart. The seed sown on rocky ground is the one who hears the word and receives it at once with joy. But he has no root and lasts only for a time. When some tribulation or persecution comes because of the word, he immediately falls away. The seed sown among thorns is the one who hears the word, but then worldly anxiety and the lure of riches choke the word and it bears no fruit. But the seed sown on rich soil is the one who hears the word and understands it, who indeed bears fruit and yields a hundred or sixty or thirtyfold."

First Reading (Isa 55:10-11)

Thus says the Lord:
Just as from the heavens
    the rain and snow come down
and do not return there
    till they have watered the earth,
    making it fertile and fruitful,
giving seed to the one who sows
    and bread to the one who eats,
so shall my word be
    that goes forth from my mouth;
my word shall not return to me void,
    but shall do my will,
    achieving the end for which I sent it.

Responsorial Psalm (Ps 65:10, 11, 12-13, 14)

℟. (Luke 8:8) The seed that falls on good ground will yield a fruitful harvest.

You have visited the land and watered it;
    greatly have you enriched it.
God's watercourses are filled;
    you have prepared the grain.

℟. The seed that falls on good ground will yield a fruitful harvest.

Thus have you prepared the land: drenching its furrows,
    breaking up its clods,
softening it with showers,
    blessing its yield.

R⁊. The seed that falls on good ground will yield a fruitful harvest.

You have crowned the year with your bounty,
    and your paths overflow with a rich harvest;
the untilled meadows overflow with it,
    and rejoicing clothes the hills.

R⁊. The seed that falls on good ground will yield a fruitful harvest.

The fields are garmented with flocks
    and the valleys blanketed with grain.
    They shout and sing for joy.

R⁊. The seed that falls on good ground will yield a fruitful harvest.

Second Reading (Rom 8:18-23)

Reflecting on Living the Gospel
The parable in today's gospel may cause us to ask, What kind of seed are we? Were we scattered on rocky soil or fertile? Will we bear fruit? If so, how much? Seed scattered on the ground does not seem to leave much room for free will. The seed scattered on rocks can scarcely move itself to the fertile soil. What about the seed that finds itself in fertile soil? Is there a responsibility to grow and produce fruit? Today, we pray for the grace to grow where we find ourselves and to produce as much fruit as possible.

Connecting the Responsorial Psalm to the Readings
Today's psalm refrain comes from the Gospel of Luke and Luke's version of the parable of the sower, "The seed that falls on good ground will yield a fruitful harvest." Within the psalm it is God who brings about fertile soil by watering the land and "breaking up its clods." God is the one who has "prepared the grain" and produced "a rich harvest." Just as fields need rich soil in order to produce crops, so it seems that we need "good ground" within ourselves in order to receive the word of God and bear its fruit. When God's word lands on this soil, the harvest will yield "a hundred or sixty or thirtyfold."

Psalmist Preparation

Perhaps we have a role to play in developing this good soil within ourselves, or maybe it is the work of the Holy Spirit inside of us gently "breaking up the clods" within our hearts to make space for this word to take root. In either case, God's word "shall not return to [him] void" as the prophet Isaiah proclaims. How do you welcome God's transforming word into your life?

Prayer

The seed is your word, O God, and Christ is the sower.
Open our eyes to see, our ears to hear, and our hearts to understand your saving Word
that we may yield a fruitful harvest for you.
God has crowned the year with goodness.
Let us shout and sing for joy. Amen.

Gospel (Matt 13:24-43
[or Matt 13:24-30]; L106A)

Jesus proposed another parable to the crowds, saying: "The kingdom of heaven may be likened to a man who sowed good seed in his field. While everyone was asleep his enemy came and sowed weeds all through the wheat, and then went off. When the crop grew and bore fruit, the weeds appeared as well. The slaves of the householder came to him and said, 'Master, did you not sow good seed in your field? Where have the weeds come from?' He answered, 'An enemy has done this.' His slaves said to him, 'Do you want us to go and pull them up?' He replied, 'No, if you pull up the weeds you might uproot the wheat along with them. Let them grow together until harvest; then at harvest time I will say to the harvesters, "First collect the weeds and tie them in bundles for burning; but gather the wheat into my barn."'"

He proposed another parable to them. "The kingdom of heaven is like a mustard seed that a person took and sowed in a field. It is the smallest of all the seeds, yet when full-grown it is the largest of plants. It becomes a large bush, and the 'birds of the sky come and dwell in its branches.'"

He spoke to them another parable. "The kingdom of heaven is like yeast that a woman took and mixed with three measures of wheat flour until the whole batch was leavened."

All these things Jesus spoke to the crowds in parables. He spoke to them only in parables, to fulfill what had been said through the prophet:

I will open my mouth in parables,
I will announce what has lain hidden from the foundation of
the world.

Then, dismissing the crowds, he went into the house. His disciples approached him and said, "Explain to us the parable of the weeds in the field." He said in reply, "He who sows good seed is the Son of Man, the field is the world, the good seed the children of the kingdom. The weeds are the children of the evil one, and the enemy who sows them is the devil. The harvest is the end of the age, and the harvesters are angels. Just as weeds are collected and burned up with fire, so will it be at the end of the age. The Son of Man will send his angels, and they will collect out of his kingdom all who cause others to sin and all evildoers. They will throw them into the fiery furnace, where there will be wailing and grinding of teeth. Then the righteous will shine like the sun in the kingdom of their Father. Whoever has ears ought to hear."

First Reading (Wis 12:13, 16-19)

There is no god besides you who have the care of all,
    that you need show you have not unjustly condemned.
For your might is the source of justice;
    your mastery over all things makes you lenient to all.
For you show your might when the perfection of your power is
      disbelieved;
    and in those who know you, you rebuke temerity.
But though you are master of might, you judge with clemency,
    and with much lenience you govern us;
    for power, whenever you will, attends you.
And you taught your people, by these deeds,
    that those who are just must be kind;
and you gave your children good ground for hope
    that you would permit repentance for their sins.

Responsorial Psalm (Ps 86:5-6, 9-10, 15-16)

R℣. (5a) Lord, you are good and forgiving.

You, O LORD, are good and forgiving,
    abounding in kindness to all who call upon you.
Hearken, O LORD, to my prayer
    and attend to the sound of my pleading.

R℣. Lord, you are good and forgiving.

All the nations you have made shall come
    and worship you, O LORD,
    and glorify your name.
For you are great, and you do wondrous deeds;
    you alone are God.

R℣. Lord, you are good and forgiving.

You, O LORD, are a God merciful and gracious,
   slow to anger, abounding in kindness and fidelity.
Turn toward me, and have pity on me;
   give your strength to your servant.

R̶/. Lord, you are good and forgiving.

Second Reading (Rom 8:26-27)

Reflecting on Living the Gospel

We learn from Jesus today that God is aware that there are weeds growing within the wheat. God is content to let them grow together, only to be separated later, at harvest time. We let God be God while we grow into the harvest we are meant to be. Our lives are not to be filled with judgmentalism but with mercy. "Let the one who is without sin cast the first stone." These are gentle reminders for us that as disciples, followers of the Son of God, we are content to allow God to act in his own time.

Connecting the Responsorial Psalm to the Readings

Like the first reading, today's psalm lifts up God as one who is "abounding in kindness" as well as "good and forgiving." In the second reading from St. Paul's letter to the Romans, we see these same traits in the Holy Trinity, who the apostle points to as our intercessor. When "we do not know how to pray as we ought," the Spirit of God comes "to the aid of our weakness" and "intercedes with inexpressible groanings."

Psalmist Preparation

When was a particular time you experienced the forgiving and healing action of God? What brought this moment about and what fruits did it produce in your life?

Prayer

Father, there is no god besides you who have the care of all
for you show your might through your mercy.
May we be just, kind, and merciful like you.
Lord, you are good and forgiving,
abounding in kindness and fidelity. Amen.

JULY 26, 2020

Gospel (Matt 13:44-52 [or Matt 13:44-46]; L109A)

Jesus said to his disciples: "The kingdom of heaven is like a treasure buried in a field, which a person finds and hides again, and out of joy goes and sells all that he has and buys that field. Again, the kingdom of heaven is like a merchant searching for fine pearls. When he finds a pearl of great price, he goes and sells all that he has and buys it. Again, the kingdom of heaven is like a net thrown into the sea, which collects fish of every kind. When it is full they haul it ashore and sit down to put what is good into buckets. What is bad they throw away. Thus it will be at the end of the age. The angels will go out and separate the wicked from the righteous and throw them into the fiery furnace, where there will be wailing and grinding of teeth.

"Do you understand all these things?" They answered, "Yes." And he replied, "Then every scribe who has been instructed in the kingdom of heaven is like the head of a household who brings from his storeroom both the new and the old."

First Reading (1 Kgs 3:5, 7-12)

The LORD appeared to Solomon in a dream at night. God said, "Ask something of me and I will give it to you." Solomon answered: "O LORD, my God, you have made me, your servant, king to succeed my father David; but I am a mere youth, not knowing at all how to act. I serve you in the midst of the people whom you have chosen, a people so vast that it cannot be numbered or counted. Give your servant, therefore, an understanding heart to judge your people and to distinguish right from wrong. For who is able to govern this vast people of yours?"

The LORD was pleased that Solomon made this request. So God said to him: "Because you have asked for this— not for a long life for yourself, nor for riches, nor for the life of your enemies, but for understanding so that you may know what is right— I do as you requested. I give you a heart so wise and understanding that there has never been anyone like you up to now, and after you there will come no one to equal you."

Responsorial Psalm (Ps 119:57, 72, 76-77, 127-128, 129-130)

℟. (97a) Lord, I love your commands.

I have said, O LORD, that my part
  is to keep your words.
The law of your mouth is to me more precious
  than thousands of gold and silver pieces.

℟. Lord, I love your commands.

Let your kindness comfort me
  according to your promise to your servants.
Let your compassion come to me that I may live,
  for your law is my delight.

℟. Lord, I love your commands.

For I love your commands
  more than gold, however fine.
For in all your precepts I go forward;
  every false way I hate.

℟. Lord, I love your commands.

Wonderful are your decrees;
  therefore I observe them.
The revelation of your words sheds light,
  giving understanding to the simple.

℟. Lord, I love your commands.

Second Reading (Rom 8:28-30)

Reflecting on Living the Gospel

The Christian life ought to be a source of joy for us. Some of this joy is reflected in the first two parables. In each, people sell whatever they can to take possession of a prized object. This is what it ought to be like for us with respect to the kingdom of heaven. Once we realize what it is, what a prize we have, we joyfully reorient all of our priorities in light of it. We want that one prize above all else. And what's more, we have it! Thus, the source of our joy.

Connecting the Responsorial Psalm to the Readings

The kingdom of God is built on the commandments to love God and to love neighbor. These are the commandments that the psalmist sings in praise of, even proclaiming them "more precious / than thousands of gold and silver pieces." For the psalmist, the law of God is the "precious pearl" and the "hidden treasure" for which he would give up everything. The prayer of Solomon is similar. When the Lord tells him, "Ask something of me and I will give it to you," Solomon does not ask for "a long life . . . / nor for riches, / nor for the life of [his] enemies." Instead Solomon tells God his greatest desire is for "an understanding heart / to judge your people and to distinguish right from wrong." Solomon would also say that knowing and keeping the law of the Lord is worth more than any earthly riches.

Psalmist Preparation

As you prepare to cantor this Sunday's psalm, take some time to consider how you reverence, make space for, and keep the word of God in your life. Would an outside observer looking in on your daily routine be able to tell this word is valuable and precious to you?

Prayer

You have given us everything that is good, O God.
Yet we desire and are distracted by things that will not last.
Teach us to seek only the treasure of serving you.
Your commands, Lord, are finer than gold,
more precious to me than silver. Amen.

Gospel (Matt 14:13-21; L112A)

When Jesus heard of the death of John the Baptist, he withdrew in a boat to a deserted place by himself. The crowds heard of this and followed him on foot from their towns. When he disembarked and saw the vast crowd, his heart was moved with pity for them, and he cured their sick. When it was evening, the disciples approached him and said, "This is a deserted place and it is already late; 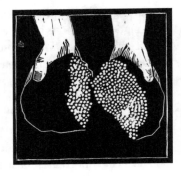 dismiss the crowds so that they can go to the villages and buy food for themselves." Jesus said to them, "There is no need for them to go away; give them some food yourselves." But they said to him, "Five loaves and two fish are all we have here." Then he said, "Bring them here to me," and he ordered the crowds to sit down on the grass. Taking the five loaves and the two fish, and looking up to heaven, he said the blessing, broke the loaves, and gave them to the disciples, who in turn gave them to the crowds. They all ate and were satisfied, and they picked up the fragments left over—twelve wicker baskets full. Those who ate were about five thousand men, not counting women and children.

First Reading (Isa 55:1-3)

Thus says the LORD:
    All you who are thirsty,
        come to the water!
    You who have no money,
        come, receive grain and eat;
    come, without paying and without cost,
        drink wine and milk!
    Why spend your money for what is not bread;
        your wages for what fails to satisfy?
    Heed me, and you shall eat well,
        you shall delight in rich fare.
    Come to me heedfully,
        listen, that you may have life.
    I will renew with you the everlasting covenant,
        the benefits assured to David.

Responsorial Psalm (Ps 145:8-9, 15-16, 17-18)

℟. (cf. 16) The hand of the Lord feeds us; he answers all our needs.

The LORD is gracious and merciful,
    slow to anger and of great kindness.
The LORD is good to all
    and compassionate toward all his works.

℟. The hand of the Lord feeds us; he answers all our needs.

The eyes of all look hopefully to you,
    and you give them their food in due season;
you open your hand
    and satisfy the desire of every living thing.

℟. The hand of the Lord feeds us; he answers all our needs.

The LORD is just in all his ways
    and holy in all his works.
The LORD is near to all who call upon him,
    to all who call upon him in truth.

℟. The hand of the Lord feeds us; he answers all our needs.

Second Reading (Rom 8:35, 37-39)

Reflecting on Living the Gospel
When we consider that Jesus multiplied the loaves so that all could eat, we recall that he acted as the prophet Elisha of old. He also foreshadowed his own Last Supper and the eucharistic gift he would leave his followers. As a result, even today we take bread, bless it, break it, and give it. In so doing we celebrate and consume Jesus himself, who was broken for us and given to us. We are sustained on our earthly journey by the Eucharist, the gift of bread multiplied, Jesus, food for the world.

Connecting the Responsorial Psalm to the Readings
Today's psalm refrain, "The hand of the Lord feeds us; he answers all our needs," summarizes the actions of Jesus in the gospel. By his own hand, the Lord of life takes up the five loaves and two fish, "said the blessing, broke the loaves, / and gave them to the disciples, / who in turn gave them to the crowds." Fed by the hand of the Lord, "all ate and were satisfied." Jesus reveals the abundance of God who calls out to his people through the prophet Isaiah, "All you who are thirsty, / come to the water! / You who have no money, / come, receive grain and eat."

EIGHTEENTH SUNDAY IN ORDINARY TIME

Whereas the disciples want to send the crowds away so they can go and "buy food for themselves," this is not Jesus' way. Our Lord is one of supreme self-giving and he continues to feed us with himself in the bread and wine of the Eucharist.

Psalmist Preparation

Throughout your own life of faith, how has Jesus fed you in his abundance? How are you being called through your ministry to be bread that is broken and shared for others?

Prayer

You feed us, Lord, not with bread alone but with your life-giving word.
Most of all you nourish us with the love of your Son, Jesus.
In his name, let us be food for others.
The hand of the Lord feeds us;
God answers all our needs. Amen.

AUGUST 9, 2020

Gospel (Matt 14:22-33; L115A)

After he had fed the people, Jesus made the disciples get into a boat and precede him to the other side, while he dismissed the crowds. After doing so, he went up on the mountain by himself to pray. When it was evening he was there alone. Meanwhile the boat, already a few miles offshore, was being tossed about by the waves, for the wind was against it. During the fourth watch of the night, he came toward them walking

on the sea. When the disciples saw him walking on the sea they were terrified. "It is a ghost," they said, and they cried out in fear. At once Jesus spoke to them, "Take courage, it is I; do not be afraid." Peter said to him in reply, "Lord, if it is you, command me to come to you on the water." He said, "Come." Peter got out of the boat and began to walk on the water toward Jesus. But when he saw how strong the wind was he became frightened; and, beginning to sink, he cried out, "Lord, save me!" Immediately Jesus stretched out his hand and caught Peter, and said to him, "O you of little faith, why did you doubt?" After they got into the boat, the wind died down. Those who were in the boat did him homage, saying, "Truly, you are the Son of God."

First Reading (1 Kgs 19:9a, 11-13a)

At the mountain of God, Horeb, Elijah came to a cave where he took shelter. Then the LORD said to him, "Go outside and stand on the mountain before the LORD; the LORD will be passing by." A strong and heavy wind was rending the mountains and crushing rocks before the LORD— but the LORD was not in the wind. After the wind there was an earthquake— but the LORD was not in the earthquake. After the earthquake there was fire— but the LORD was not in the fire. After the fire there was a tiny whispering sound. When he heard this, Elijah hid his face in his cloak and went and stood at the entrance of the cave.

Responsorial Psalm (Ps 85:9, 10, 11-12, 13-14)

R℣. (8) Lord, let us see your kindness, and grant us your salvation.

I will hear what God proclaims;
  the LORD—for he proclaims peace.
Near indeed is his salvation to those who fear him,
  glory dwelling in our land.

R℣. Lord, let us see your kindness, and grant us your salvation.

Kindness and truth shall meet;
  justice and peace shall kiss.
Truth shall spring out of the earth,
  and justice shall look down from heaven.

R℣. Lord, let us see your kindness, and grant us your salvation.

The LORD himself will give his benefits;
  our land shall yield its increase.
Justice shall walk before him,
  and prepare the way of his steps.

R℣. Lord, let us see your kindness, and grant us your salvation.

Second Reading (Rom 9:1-5)

Reflecting on Living the Gospel

When we, like the disciples in the boat from today's gospel, experience turbulence and storms, we may be reassured that the Lord is near. When we call, he answers. He will join us and the storms will subside. Is it any wonder this story has been read for centuries as an allegory for the relationship between Christ and the church? The boat may protect us from the storm, but we still experience the effects of the storm. It is only Jesus himself who can calm the waters, and then he himself joins us in the boat.

Connecting the Responsorial Psalm to the Readings

The experiences of both Elijah and the disciples in today's gospel offer us opportunities to "see" God's kindness. As the psalmist states, "I will hear what God proclaims; / the Lord—for he proclaims peace." In the "tiny whispering sound" and the calm waters after the storm, God's peace is announced.

Psalmist Preparation

Where do you find time and space to meet God in silence so as to be rooted in his kindness and salvation?

Prayer

You chose to make your presence known in the tiniest whispering sound.
When wind and quake, fire and storm threaten us,
command us, Lord, to come to you and wait for your saving word.
I will hear what God proclaims:
peace, salvation, kindness, truth. Amen.

Gospel (Luke 1:39-56; L622)

Mary set out and traveled to the hill country in haste to a town of Judah, where she entered the house of Zechariah and greeted Elizabeth. When Elizabeth heard Mary's greeting, the infant leaped in her womb, and Elizabeth, filled with the Holy Spirit, cried out in a loud voice and said, "Blessed are you among women, and blessed is the fruit of your womb. And how does this hap-

pen to me, that the mother of my Lord should come to me? For at the moment the sound of your greeting reached my ears, the infant in my womb leaped for joy. Blessed are you who believed that what was spoken to you by the Lord would be fulfilled."

And Mary said:

"My soul proclaims the greatness of the Lord;
    my spirit rejoices in God my Savior
    for he has looked with favor upon his lowly servant.
From this day all generations will call me blessed:
    the Almighty has done great things for me,
    and holy is his Name.
He has mercy on those who fear him
    in every generation.
He has shown the strength of his arm,
    and has scattered the proud in their conceit.
He has cast down the mighty from their thrones,
    and has lifted up the lowly.
He has filled the hungry with good things,
    and the rich he has sent away empty.
He has come to the help of his servant Israel
    for he has remembered his promise of mercy,
    the promise he made to our fathers,
    to Abraham and his children forever."

Mary remained with her about three months and then returned to her home.

First Reading (Rev 11:19a; 12:1-6a, 10ab)

God's temple in heaven was opened, and the ark of his covenant could be seen in the temple.

A great sign appeared in the sky, a woman clothed with the sun, with the moon beneath her feet, and on her head a crown of twelve stars. She was with child and wailed aloud in pain as she labored to give birth. Then another sign appeared in the sky; it was a huge red dragon, with seven heads and ten horns, and on its heads were seven diadems. Its tail swept away a third of the stars in the sky and hurled them down to the earth. Then the dragon stood before the woman about to give birth, to devour her child when she gave birth. She gave birth to a son, a male child, destined to rule all the nations with an iron rod. Her child was caught up to God and his throne. The woman herself fled into the desert where she had a place prepared by God.

Then I heard a loud voice in heaven say:
> "Now have salvation and power come,
>> and the Kingdom of our God
>> and the authority of his Anointed One."

Responsorial Psalm (Ps 45:10, 11, 12, 16)

℟. (10bc) The queen stands at your right hand, arrayed in gold.

The queen takes her place at your right hand in gold of Ophir.

℟. The queen stands at your right hand, arrayed in gold.

Hear, O daughter, and see; turn your ear,
> forget your people and your father's house.

℟. The queen stands at your right hand, arrayed in gold.

So shall the king desire your beauty;
> for he is your lord.

℟. The queen stands at your right hand, arrayed in gold.

They are borne in with gladness and joy;
> they enter the palace of the king.

℟. The queen stands at your right hand, arrayed in gold.

See Appendix, p. 208, for Second Reading

ASSUMPTION OF THE BLESSED VIRGIN MARY

Reflecting on Living the Gospel

We hear Mary's voice in the Gospel of Luke today. Luke is the evangelist who gives the largest role to Mary, from the annunciation where Mary said "yes," and the visitation, the nativity of Jesus, and even to her own presence at significant times in Jesus' ministry through Pentecost in Acts of the Apostles. As mother of Jesus, or "mother of my Lord," as Elizabeth calls her, Mary was certainly in a unique position. She had a vision for justice that certainly would have inspired and informed Jesus. May her vision inspire us, the disciples of her son, as well.

Connecting the Responsorial Psalm to the Readings

Today's psalm gives us a vision of a queen "arrayed in gold" standing at the right hand of the king. In the gospel, we find a very different picture of Mary, the Mother of God. Instead of gold, we could imagine she's wearing traveling clothes. Instead of standing in a throne room, she enters the house of her kinswoman Elizabeth. And the king she accompanies, rather than being a ruler with wealth and power, is an unborn baby just beginning to grow in her womb. We might wonder, how do these two images coexist, the queen arrayed in gold and the young peasant woman from Nazareth? Mary gives us the key herself when she proclaims that God "has cast down the mighty from their thrones, / and has lifted up the lowly." In the kingdom of heaven, it is the poor and the lowly who are "borne in with gladness and joy."

Psalmist Preparation

In the *Magnificat*, Mary shows us that the way to enter into the kingdom of God is the way of humility, peace, and justice. How are you being called to emulate the queenship of Mary?

Prayer

O God, in Mary, you reveal your promise to all your people.
Array us with the splendor of her faithfulness
that we may enter your courts with gladness and joy.
My soul proclaims the greatness of the Lord;
my spirit rejoices in God my savior. Amen.

AUGUST 16, 2020

Gospel (Matt 15:21-28; L118A)

At that time, Jesus withdrew to the region of Tyre and Sidon. And behold, a Canaanite woman of that district came and called out, "Have pity on me, Lord, Son of David! My daughter is tormented by a demon." But Jesus did not say a word in answer to her. Jesus' disciples came and asked him, "Send her away, for she keeps calling out after us." He said in reply, "I was sent only to the lost sheep of the house of Israel." But the  woman came and did Jesus homage, saying, "Lord, help me." He said in reply, "It is not right to take the food of the children and throw it to the dogs." She said, "Please, Lord, for even the dogs eat the scraps that fall from the table of their masters." Then Jesus said to her in reply, "O woman, great is your faith! Let it be done for you as you wish." And the woman's daughter was healed from that hour.

First Reading (Isa 56:1, 6-7)

Thus says the LORD:
>Observe what is right, do what is just;
>>for my salvation is about to come,
>>my justice, about to be revealed.

>The foreigners who join themselves to the LORD,
>>ministering to him,
>loving the name of the LORD,
>>and becoming his servants—
>all who keep the sabbath free from profanation
>>and hold to my covenant,
>them I will bring to my holy mountain
>>and make joyful in my house of prayer;
>their burnt offerings and sacrifices
>>will be acceptable on my altar,
>for my house shall be called
>>a house of prayer for all peoples.

Responsorial Psalm (Ps 67:2-3, 5, 6, 8)

R℣. (4) O God, let all the nations praise you!

May God have pity on us and bless us;
  may he let his face shine upon us.
So may your way be known upon earth;
  among all nations, your salvation.

R℣. O God, let all the nations praise you!

May the nations be glad and exult
  because you rule the peoples in equity;
  the nations on the earth you guide.

R℣. O God, let all the nations praise you!

May the peoples praise you, O God;
  may all the peoples praise you!
May God bless us,
  and may all the ends of the earth fear him!

R℣. O God, let all the nations praise you!

Second Reading (Rom 11:13-15, 29-32)

Reflecting on Living the Gospel

The resurrection gives power and new life. After the resurrection, Jesus tells his disciples to go to all nations, teaching and baptizing. The scene from today's gospel lets us know that the earthly ministry of Jesus was not characterized in that way, at least not as Matthew presents it. But now that Christ has been raised from the dead, all are welcome, and all may be disciples. No longer is God's chosen people limited to one group. Instead, by what God has done in Christ, all are chosen and called to be children of God.

Connecting the Responsorial Psalm to the Readings

Although the Old Testament is the story of God specifically joining himself to the people of Israel, all throughout the Hebrew Scriptures we find the understanding that their God is not the ruler of their people alone, but of the whole earth. Today's psalm refrain, "O God, let all the nations praise you!" speaks to this.

Psalmist Preparation

The book of Psalms is sacred to both the Jewish and the Christian people. All over the world, Jews and Christians pray with the words of the psalms in their personal prayer and in communal liturgy. As a cantor, you have a role in proclaiming the psalms to the people of God that links you closely with our Jewish brothers and sisters. How do the psalms sustain and nourish you in faith?

Prayer

Those the world rejects, Lord—the stranger, the foreigner,
the one who disrupts our daily routine—are first to receive your mercy.
Grant us their great faith in you.
O God, let all the nations praise you!
May all the peoples praise you, O God. Amen.

Gospel (Matt 16:13-20; L121A)

Jesus went into the region of Caesarea Philippi and he asked his disciples, "Who do people say that the Son of Man is?" They replied, "Some say John the Baptist, others Elijah, still others Jeremiah or one of the prophets." He said to them, "But who do you say that I am?" Simon Peter said in reply, "You are the Christ, the Son of the living God." Jesus said to him in reply, "Blessed are you,  Simon son of Jonah. For flesh and blood has not revealed this to you, but my heavenly Father. And so I say to you, you are Peter, and upon this rock I will build my church, and the gates of the netherworld shall not prevail against it. I will give you the keys to the kingdom of heaven. Whatever you bind on earth shall be bound in heaven; and whatever you loose on earth shall be loosed in heaven." Then he strictly ordered his disciples to tell no one that he was the Christ.

First Reading (Isa 22:19-23)

Thus says the LORD to Shebna, master of the palace:
"I will thrust you from your office
and pull you down from your station.
On that day I will summon my servant
Eliakim, son of Hilkiah;
I will clothe him with your robe,
and gird him with your sash,
and give over to him your authority.
He shall be a father to the inhabitants of Jerusalem,
and to the house of Judah.
I will place the key of the House of David on Eliakim's shoulder;
when he opens, no one shall shut;
when he shuts, no one shall open.
I will fix him like a peg in a sure spot,
to be a place of honor for his family."

Responsorial Psalm (Ps 138:1-2, 2-3, 6, 8)

℞. (8bc) Lord, your love is eternal; do not forsake the work of your hands.

I will give thanks to you, O LORD, with all my heart,
    for you have heard the words of my mouth;
in the presence of the angels I will sing your praise;
    I will worship at your holy temple.

℞. Lord, your love is eternal; do not forsake the work of your hands.

I will give thanks to your name,
    because of your kindness and your truth:
when I called, you answered me;
    you built up strength within me.

℞. Lord, your love is eternal; do not forsake the work of your hands.

The LORD is exalted, yet the lowly he sees,
    and the proud he knows from afar.
Your kindness, O LORD, endures forever;
    forsake not the work of your hands.

℞. Lord, your love is eternal; do not forsake the work of your hands.

Second Reading (Rom 11:33-36)

Reflecting on Living the Gospel

Simon Barjonah confesses Jesus as the Christ and recognizes him for who he is. Jesus responds by saying this insight was given to him by the Heavenly Father. Jesus then names him "Peter," a Greek term meaning "Rock" (in Aramaic the term is *Kephas*). Jesus then says that on this "rock," he will build his "church." The term "church" appears in the gospels only in Matthew, and only here and in Matthew 18:17. Matthew is reminding his audience that Peter was a spokesperson for the group and confessed Jesus as Christ. Yet even this confession was not due to his own insight but was a gift of the Father.

Connecting the Responsorial Psalm to the Readings

Today's psalm refrain speaks to the one in whom our hope lies: "Lord, your love is eternal; do not forsake the work of your hands." Despite the many times the people of Israel turn away from God in the Old Testament, God continues to call them back into relationship with him. This is true with the disciples and the early church in the New Testament as well. In the verses immediately following today's gospel (which will be proclaimed next Sunday), Peter protests Jesus' revelation that he will be killed and then raised, which leads to the harsh rebuke, "Get behind me, Satan! You are an obstacle to me."

Psalmist Preparation

In your own life of faith, when have you stumbled and fallen? In these moments have you perceived God at your side with his eternal love, ready to redeem and restore?

Prayer

You give your church authority, O God, not to rule by fear or might but to loosen the chains of death and to bind us all to your Son.
Teach us to use our power wisely.
In the presence of the angels I will sing your praise;
I will worship at your holy temple. Amen.

AUGUST 30, 2020

Gospel (Matt 16:21-27; L124A)

Jesus began to show his disciples that he must go to Jerusalem and suffer greatly from the elders, the chief priests, and the scribes, and be killed and on the third day be raised. Then Peter took Jesus aside and began to rebuke him, "God forbid, Lord! No such thing shall ever happen to you." He turned and said to Peter, "Get behind me, Satan! You are an obstacle to me. You are thinking not as God does, but as human beings do."

Then Jesus said to his disciples, "Whoever wishes to come after me must deny himself, take up his cross, and follow me. For whoever wishes to save his life will lose it, but whoever loses his life for my sake will find it. What profit would there be for one to gain the whole world and forfeit his life? Or what can one give in exchange for his life? For the Son of Man will come with his angels in his Father's glory, and then he will repay all according to his conduct."

First Reading (Jer 20:7-9)

You duped me, O Lord, and I let myself be duped;
> you were too strong for me, and you triumphed.
All the day I am an object of laughter;
> everyone mocks me.

Whenever I speak, I must cry out,
> violence and outrage is my message;
the word of the Lord has brought me
> derision and reproach all the day.

I say to myself, I will not mention him,
> I will speak in his name no more.
But then it becomes like fire burning in my heart,
> imprisoned in my bones;
I grow weary holding it in, I cannot endure it.

Responsorial Psalm (Ps 63:2, 3-4, 5-6, 8-9)

R℣. (2b) My soul is thirsting for you, O Lord my God.

O God, you are my God whom I seek;
    for you my flesh pines and my soul thirsts
    like the earth, parched, lifeless and without water.

R℣. My soul is thirsting for you, O Lord my God.

Thus have I gazed toward you in the sanctuary
    to see your power and your glory,
for your kindness is a greater good than life;
    my lips shall glorify you.

R℣. My soul is thirsting for you, O Lord my God.

Thus will I bless you while I live;
    lifting up my hands, I will call upon your name.
As with the riches of a banquet shall my soul be satisfied,
    and with exultant lips my mouth shall praise you.

R℣. My soul is thirsting for you, O Lord my God.

You are my help,
    and in the shadow of your wings I shout for joy.
My soul clings fast to you;
    your right hand upholds me.

R℣. My soul is thirsting for you, O Lord my God.

Second Reading (Rom 12:1-2)

Reflecting on Living the Gospel

The paradoxical sayings of Jesus are on full display today, following Peter's proclamation of him as Messiah. The paradoxes come to the fore because of Peter's misunderstanding of what it means to be the Messiah. Rather than victory and a glorious reign (which is what Peter had in mind), Jesus rebukes him to say that his Messiahship will lead to his death. Only then will he be raised. As disciples, we are to take on the mind of God, to think not as human beings do. When we think as God does, we will know that loss means finding, denial of oneself is ultimate fulfillment, and death leads to life.

Connecting the Responsorial Psalm to the Readings

The question could be asked, if this is the way of God that suffering, struggle, and ultimately death are all a part of the package, what has kept Jews and Christians faithful throughout the ages? Today's psalm refrain seems to hold an answer: "My soul is thirsting for you, O Lord my God." Just as we need water to live, our longing for God is innate and undeniable. We may try to satisfy the thirst in our souls with many other things, but ultimately true peace is only found in our Creator.

Psalmist Preparation

How do you experience the thirst for God in your life?

Prayer

Lord, our hearts desire to follow you, yet our thoughts keep counting the cost.
Captivate us with your mercy that we may conform our minds to Christ to discern what is good, pleasing, and perfect.
I will bless you while I live;
with exultant lips my mouth shall praise you. Amen.

Gospel (Matt 18:15-20; L127A)

Jesus said to his disciples: "If your brother sins against you, go and tell him his fault between you and him alone. If he listens to you, you have won over your brother. If he does not listen, take one or two others along with you, so that 'every fact may be established on the testimony of two or three witnesses.' If he refuses to listen to them, tell the church. If he refuses to listen even to the church, then treat him as you would a Gentile or a tax collector. Amen, I say to you, whatever you bind on earth shall be bound in heaven, and whatever you loose on earth shall be loosed in heaven. Again, amen, I say to you, if two of you agree on earth about anything for which they are to pray, it shall be granted to them by my heavenly Father. For where two or three are gathered together in my name, there am I in the midst of them."

First Reading (Ezek 33:7-9)

Thus says the LORD:
>   You, son of man, I have appointed watchman for the house of Israel;
>   when you hear me say anything, you shall warn them for me.

If I tell the wicked, "O wicked one, you shall surely die,"
>   and you do not speak out to dissuade the wicked from his way,
>   the wicked shall die for his guilt,
>   but I will hold you responsible for his death.

But if you warn the wicked,
>   trying to turn him from his way,
>   and he refuses to turn from his way,
>   he shall die for his guilt,
>   but you shall save yourself.

Responsorial Psalm (Ps 95:1-2, 6-7, 8-9)

℟. (8) If today you hear his voice, harden not your hearts.

Come, let us sing joyfully to the LORD;
>   let us acclaim the rock of our salvation.

Let us come into his presence with thanksgiving;
>   let us joyfully sing psalms to him.

℟. If today you hear his voice, harden not your hearts.

Come, let us bow down in worship;
    let us kneel before the LORD who made us.
For he is our God,
    and we are the people he shepherds, the flock he guides.

Ry. If today you hear his voice, harden not your hearts.

Oh, that today you would hear his voice:
    "Harden not your hearts as at Meribah,
    as in the day of Massah in the desert,
where your fathers tempted me;
    they tested me though they had seen my works."

Ry. If today you hear his voice, harden not your hearts.

Second Reading (Rom 13:8-10)

Reflecting on Living the Gospel

Wouldn't life be so much better if we could all live in peace and happiness? But relationships are not like that. Even the most secure and safe nuclear families—individuals raised in the same household, for whom love may be a given—have challenges with one another. The church is the same. In the face of this, Matthew gives us some practical steps to follow. Only when we experience the new life of the resurrection will every tear be wiped away, and relationships restored. Until that time, we do the best we can, motivated by love and guided by the wisdom of Christ.

Connecting the Responsorial Psalm to the Readings

Today's psalm tells us what is needed in order to live well in a community of peace and reconciliation. Sometimes God's messages of correction and encouragement will come from the mouths of our brothers and sisters in Christ. When this happens our psalm refrain urges us, "[H]arden not your hearts." A heart that is filled up with pride and vanity, or is fearful of being cast out, cannot open and soften to accept correction. When we are secure in God's love and our own preciousness in his sight, we can let go of pride and anger. Only then can we take feedback with the goodwill it was intended and strive to be better as we continue on the journey of faith.

Psalmist Preparation

How do you keep your heart open and accepting to God's correcting word?

Prayer

How easy it is to complain about another, to gossip or slander, defame or despise.

Yet you have made us one family, Lord, bound together by love.

In Christ may we be reconciled.

Come, let us sing joyfully to the Lord;

let us acclaim the rock of our salvation. Amen.

Gospel (Matt 18:21-35; L130A)

Peter approached Jesus and asked him, "Lord, if my brother sins against me, how often must I forgive? As many as seven times?" Jesus answered, "I say to you, not seven times but seventy-seven times. That is why the kingdom of heaven may be likened to a king who decided to settle accounts with his servants. When he began the accounting, a debtor was brought before him who owed him a huge amount. Since he had  no way of paying it back, his master ordered him to be sold, along with his wife, his children, and all his property, in payment of the debt. At that, the servant fell down, did him homage, and said, 'Be patient with me, and I will pay you back in full.' Moved with compassion the master of that servant let him go and forgave him the loan. When that servant had left, he found one of his fellow servants who owed him a much smaller amount. He seized him and started to choke him, demanding, 'Pay back what you owe.' Falling to his knees, his fellow servant begged him, 'Be patient with me, and I will pay you back.' But he refused. Instead, he had the fellow servant put in prison until he paid back the debt. Now when his fellow servants saw what had happened, they were deeply disturbed, and went to their master and reported the whole affair. His master summoned him and said to him, 'You wicked servant! I forgave you your entire debt because you begged me to. Should you not have had pity on your fellow servant, as I had pity on you?' Then in anger his master handed him over to the torturers until he should pay back the whole debt. So will my heavenly Father do to you, unless each of you forgives your brother from your heart."

First Reading (Sir 27:30–28:7)

Wrath and anger are hateful things,
    yet the sinner hugs them tight.
The vengeful will suffer the LORD's vengeance,
    for he remembers their sins in detail.
Forgive your neighbor's injustice;
    then when you pray, your own sins will be forgiven.

Could anyone nourish anger against another
   and expect healing from the LORD?
Could anyone refuse mercy to another like himself,
   can he seek pardon for his own sins?
If one who is but flesh cherishes wrath,
   who will forgive his sins?
Remember your last days, set enmity aside;
   remember death and decay, and cease from sin!
Think of the commandments, hate not your neighbor;
   remember the Most High's covenant, and overlook faults.

Responsorial Psalm (Ps 103:1-2, 3-4, 9-10, 11-12)

R̖. (8) The Lord is kind and merciful, slow to anger, and rich in compassion.

Bless the LORD, O my soul;
   and all my being, bless his holy name.
Bless the LORD, O my soul,
   and forget not all his benefits.

R̖. The Lord is kind and merciful, slow to anger, and rich in compassion.

He pardons all your iniquities,
   heals all your ills,
redeems your life from destruction,
   he crowns you with kindness and compassion.

R̖. The Lord is kind and merciful, slow to anger, and rich in compassion.

He will not always chide,
   nor does he keep his wrath forever.
Not according to our sins does he deal with us,
   nor does he requite us according to our crimes.

R̖. The Lord is kind and merciful, slow to anger, and rich in compassion.

For as the heavens are high above the earth,
   so surpassing is his kindness toward those who fear him.
As far as the east is from the west,
   so far has he put our transgressions from us.

R̖. The Lord is kind and merciful, slow to anger, and rich in compassion.

Second Reading (Rom 14:7-9)

Reflecting on Living the Gospel

Grudges are awful things. But today's gospel calls us to a higher standard. The forgiveness we've experienced should motivate us to be free with forgiveness when others wrong us. We cannot dole out forgiveness in infinitesimal pieces only to those we deem worthy. Instead, forgiveness ought to be given freely. We must die to the grudges, slights, rudeness, and other transgressions we've suffered and rise to a sense of freedom that comes through forgiving as we've been forgiven. Jesus himself warns us that if we withhold forgiveness, it will be withheld from us. And the consequences of that are severe indeed.

Connecting the Responsorial Psalm to the Readings

We have been created in the image and likeness of God and are called to be like him. Today's psalm refrain proclaims, "The Lord is kind and merciful, slow to anger, and rich in compassion." This is the ideal to which we are all to aspire. To become "rich in compassion," we must first experience and sit in the compassionate love of God, the one who "pardons all your iniquities, / heals all your ills, / redeems your life from destruction," and "crowns you with kindness and compassion." In today's parable it seems that the debtor who was forgiven "a huge amount" did not let the experience of the king's generosity to him pierce his soul. When he is called upon to be generous and compassionate, he responds instead with anger and revenge.

Psalmist Preparation

In order to proclaim God's mercy and kindness to others, take a moment in prayer to consider how you have experienced this mercy and compassion in your own life. Where might God be calling you to exercise forgiveness in your relationships with others?

Prayer

Father, you are slow to anger and rich in compassion.
In your mercy, we ask you,
forgive us our sins as we forgive those who sin against us.
Bless the Lord, O my soul;
and all my being, bless God's holy name. Amen.

Gospel (Matt 20:1-16a; L133A)

Jesus told his disciples this parable: "The kingdom of heaven is like a land-owner who went out at dawn to hire laborers for his vineyard. After agreeing with them for the usual daily wage, he sent them into his vineyard. Going out about nine o'clock, the landowner saw others standing idle in the marketplace, and he said to them, 'You too go into my vineyard, and I will give you what is just.' So they went off. And he went out again around noon, and around three o'clock, and did likewise. Going out about five o'clock, the land-owner found others standing around, and said to them, 'Why do you stand here idle all day?' They answered, 'Because no one has hired us.' He said to them, 'You too go into my vineyard.' When it was evening the owner of the vineyard said to his foreman, 'Summon the laborers and give them their pay, beginning with the last and ending with the first.' When those who had started about five o'clock came, each received the usual daily wage. So when the first came, they thought that they would receive more, but each of them also got the usual wage. And on receiving it they grumbled against the landowner, saying, 'These last ones worked only one hour, and you have made them equal to us, who bore the day's burden and the heat.' He said to one of them in reply, 'My friend, I am not cheating you. Did you not agree with me for the usual daily wage? Take what is yours and go. What if I wish to give this last one the same as you? Or am I not free to do as I wish with my own money? Are you envious because I am generous?' Thus, the last will be first, and the first will be last."

First Reading (Isa 55:6-9)

Seek the LORD while he may be found,
call him while he is near.
Let the scoundrel forsake his way,
and the wicked his thoughts;
let him turn to the LORD for mercy;
to our God, who is generous in forgiving.
For my thoughts are not your thoughts,
nor are your ways my ways, says the LORD.

As high as the heavens are above the earth,
    so high are my ways above your ways
    and my thoughts above your thoughts.

Responsorial Psalm (Ps 145:2-3, 8-9, 17-18)

℟. (18a) The Lord is near to all who call upon him.

Every day will I bless you,
    and I will praise your name forever and ever.
Great is the LORD and highly to be praised;
    his greatness is unsearchable.

℟. The Lord is near to all who call upon him.

The LORD is gracious and merciful,
    slow to anger and of great kindness.
The LORD is good to all
    and compassionate toward all his works.

℟. The Lord is near to all who call upon him.

The LORD is just in all his ways
    and holy in all his works.
The LORD is near to all who call upon him,
    to all who call upon him in truth.

℟. The Lord is near to all who call upon him.

Second Reading (Phil 1:20c-24, 27a)

Reflecting on Living the Gospel

When we see acts of generosity, it can be natural to expect that we might receive some of that generosity as well. It might sound strange to hear it said that someone is generous only with one group and not another. And such is the seeming riddle of today's parable. God is a just and generous giver. When we receive what we have from God, there is no room for complaint, jealousy, or envy. Let us die to our own sense of who is just and worthy in God's sight and leave room to be surprised by his generosity.

Connecting the Responsorial Psalm to the Readings

Today's psalm refrain proclaims, "The Lord is near to all who call upon him." There is an inherent gift and challenge within this line. We are reassured of God's help and nearness to us at all times, especially when we are in need. And we also must proclaim with words and actions that this is true for everyone else too. For God, there is no "us and them." Each person he has created is beloved and precious in his sight, including those who have hurt us. Our greatest prayer should be that those who do evil will be converted. As Isaiah says in our first reading, "Let the scoundrel forsake his way, / and the wicked his thoughts; / let him turn to the Lord for mercy."

Psalmist Preparation

Sometimes it seems much easier to desire the downfall or condemnation of those who wreak havoc on the world. But this is not God's dream. Instead, he desires to gather all people to himself. Let us take time to pray this week that all people would turn toward the Lord and enter into the kingdom of God.

Prayer

You are gracious and compassionate to all who call you, Lord,
generous to the least among us and faithful to all.
Help us rejoice in your merciful love.
Every day will I bless you,
and I will praise your name forever. Amen.

Gospel (Matt 21:28-32; L136A)

Jesus said to the chief priests and elders of the people: "What is your opinion? A man had two sons. He came to the first and said, 'Son, go out and work in the vineyard today.' He said in reply, 'I will not,' but afterwards changed his mind and went. The man came to the other son and gave the same order. He said in reply, 'Yes, sir,' but did not go. Which of the two did his father's will?" They answered, "The first." Jesus said to them, "Amen, I  say to you, tax collectors and prostitutes are entering the kingdom of God before you. When John came to you in the way of righteousness, you did not believe him; but tax collectors and prostitutes did. Yet even when you saw that, you did not later change your minds and believe him."

First Reading (Ezek 18:25-28)

Thus says the Lord:
You say, "The Lord's way is not fair!"
Hear now, house of Israel:
    Is it my way that is unfair, or rather, are not your ways unfair?
When someone virtuous turns away from virtue to commit iniquity,
        and dies,
    it is because of the iniquity he committed that he must die.
But if he turns from the wickedness he has committed,
        and does what is right and just,
        he shall preserve his life;
    since he has turned away from all the sins that he has committed,
        he shall surely live, he shall not die.

Responsorial Psalm (Ps 25:4-5, 6-7, 8-9)

R℣. (6a) Remember your mercies, O Lord.

Your ways, O Lord, make known to me;
    teach me your paths,
guide me in your truth and teach me,
    for you are God my savior.

R℣. Remember your mercies, O Lord.

Remember that your compassion, O LORD,
   and your love are from of old.
The sins of my youth and my frailties remember not;
   in your kindness remember me,
      because of your goodness, O LORD.

R℣. Remember your mercies, O Lord.

Good and upright is the LORD;
   thus he shows sinners the way.
He guides the humble to justice,
   and teaches the humble his way.

R℣. Remember your mercies, O Lord.

Second Reading (Phil 2:1-11 [or Phil 2:1-5])

Reflecting on Living the Gospel

Have you ever met a flatterer, or people pleaser? One who says what you want to hear but has no intention of following through? Or one who over-promises and under-delivers? It can be challenging to hear the words of Jesus in the parable today about such behaviors. Despite our best intentions, it is our actions that truly mean more than our words. There are many reasons why we might over-promise, but we are reminded of another saying in the gospels, "Let your 'Yes' mean 'Yes' and your 'No' mean 'No'" (Matt 5:37). This is simply good advice from Jesus the teacher.

Connecting the Responsorial Psalm to the Readings

Today's psalm is one of a repentant sinner who begs for God to forget "the sins of my youth and my frailties." It reminds us that we are all repentant sinners who turn to the Lord, humbly seeking mercy. Only in emptying ourselves of our pride and sureness (the same things that block the chief priests and elders of today's gospel in recognizing Jesus' identity) can we become the humble who can learn the ways of God. We find our greatest model of humility in Jesus. St. Paul's letter to the Philippians reminds us of how "he emptied himself, / taking the form of a slave, / coming in human likeness; / and found human in appearance, / he humbled himself, / becoming obedient to the point of death, / even death on a cross."

Psalmist Preparation

Just as the psalmist asks for God to "[r]emember your mercies, O Lord," let us also take time this week in prayer to contemplate the compassion God has shown throughout our lives.

Prayer

We grumble in our selfishness, Lord, and place ourselves above others.
But you call us to turn away from our sin
that we may turn in love to you and do your will.
Your ways, O Lord, make known to me;
teach me your paths. Amen.

Gospel (Matt 21:33-43; L139A)

Jesus said to the chief priests and the elders of the people: "Hear another parable. There was a landowner who planted a vineyard, put a hedge around it, dug a wine press in it, and built a tower. Then he leased it to tenants and went on a journey. When vintage time drew near, he sent his servants to the tenants to obtain his produce. But the tenants seized the servants and one they beat, another they killed, and a third they stoned. Again he sent other servants, more numerous than the first ones, but they treated them in the same way. Finally, he sent his son to them, thinking, 'They will respect my son.' But when the tenants saw the son, they said to one another, 'This is the heir. Come, let us kill him and acquire his inheritance.' They seized him, threw him out of the vineyard, and killed him. What will the owner of the vineyard do to those tenants when he comes?" They answered him, "He will put those wretched men to a wretched death and lease his vineyard to other tenants who will give him the produce at the proper times." Jesus said to them, "Did you never read in the Scriptures:

> *The stone that the builders rejected*
> *has become the cornerstone;*
> *by the Lord has this been done,*
> *and it is wonderful in our eyes?*

Therefore, I say to you, the kingdom of God will be taken away from you and given to a people that will produce its fruit."

First Reading (Isa 5:1-7)

> Let me now sing of my friend,
> my friend's song concerning his vineyard.
> My friend had a vineyard
> on a fertile hillside;
> he spaded it, cleared it of stones,
> and planted the choicest vines;
> within it he built a watchtower,
> and hewed out a wine press.
> Then he looked for the crop of grapes,
> but what it yielded was wild grapes.

Now, inhabitants of Jerusalem and people of Judah,
    judge between me and my vineyard:
What more was there to do for my vineyard
    that I had not done?
Why, when I looked for the crop of grapes,
    did it bring forth wild grapes?
Now, I will let you know
    what I mean to do with my vineyard:
take away its hedge, give it to grazing,
    break through its wall, let it be trampled!
Yes, I will make it a ruin:
    it shall not be pruned or hoed,
    but overgrown with thorns and briers;
I will command the clouds
    not to send rain upon it.
The vineyard of the LORD of hosts is the house of Israel,
    and the people of Judah are his cherished plant;
he looked for judgment, but see, bloodshed!
    for justice, but hark, the outcry!

Responsorial Psalm (Ps 80:9, 12, 13-14, 15-16, 19-20)

R̸. (Isaiah 5:7a) The vineyard of the Lord is the house of Israel.

A vine from Egypt you transplanted;
    you drove away the nations and planted it.
It put forth its foliage to the Sea,
    its shoots as far as the River.

R̸. The vineyard of the Lord is the house of Israel.

Why have you broken down its walls,
    so that every passer-by plucks its fruit,
the boar from the forest lays it waste,
    and the beasts of the field feed upon it?

R̸. The vineyard of the Lord is the house of Israel.

Once again, O LORD of hosts,
    look down from heaven, and see;
take care of this vine,
    and protect what your right hand has planted,
    the son of man whom you yourself made strong.

R̸. The vineyard of the Lord is the house of Israel.

Then we will no more withdraw from you;
> give us new life, and we will call upon your name.

O Lᴏʀᴅ, God of hosts, restore us;
> if your face shine upon us, then we shall be saved.

R℣. The vineyard of the Lord is the house of Israel.

Second Reading (Phil 4:6-9)

Reflecting on Living the Gospel

Though this gospel reading was written two thousand years ago, it unfortunately has been misused throughout history as justification for Christians to persecute Jews. The church tells us that the words here echo words of the prophets and their critiques of the people of God. But when Christians definitively separated from Jews, the words were understood differently, not as an internal critique between members of a family but as a forceful condemnation of the "other." Now in the modern world, especially in light of the holocaust, we must do all we can to put away any anti-Jewish reading of the text. In so doing, we will walk in newness of life.

Connecting the Responsorial Psalm to the Readings

Today's psalm could be seen as a direct response to the devastating first reading from the prophet Isaiah where God vows to let his vineyard ("the house of Israel") be "overgrown with thorns and briars." The psalmist pleads, "Once again, O Lord of hosts, / look down from heaven, and see; / take care of this vine, / and protect what your right hand has planted."

Psalmist Preparation

The writings of the prophets, like the parables of Jesus, are meant to shake us from our complacency and cause us to take stock of life. In the psalms we find prayers for every emotion, from triumphant and praising, to pleading and invoking. Which psalms speak to you most at this time in your life?

Prayer

You have planted in our hearts, O God, the seed of your Word
and have tended it with your merciful care.
May we be good stewards of your grace.
O Lord, God of hosts, restore us;
shine your face upon us, and we shall be saved. *Amen.*

Gospel (Matt 22:1-14 [or Matt 22:1-10]; L142A)

Jesus again in reply spoke to the chief priests and elders of the people in parables, saying, "The kingdom of heaven may be likened to a king who gave a wedding feast for his son. He dispatched his servants to summon the invited guests to the feast, but they refused to come. A second time he sent other servants, saying, 'Tell those invited: "Behold, I have prepared my banquet, my calves and fattened cattle are killed, and everything is ready; come to the feast."' Some ignored the invitation and went away, one to his farm, another to his business. The rest laid hold of his servants, mistreated them, and killed them. The king was enraged and sent his troops, destroyed those murderers, and burned their city. Then he said to his servants, 'The feast is ready, but those who were invited were not worthy to come. Go out, therefore, into the main roads and invite to the feast whomever you find.' The servants went out into the streets and gathered all they found, bad and good alike, and the hall was filled with guests. But when the king came in to meet the guests, he saw a man there not dressed in a wedding garment. The king said to him, 'My friend, how is it that you came in here without a wedding garment?' But he was reduced to silence. Then the king said to his attendants, 'Bind his hands and feet, and cast him into the darkness outside, where there will be wailing and grinding of teeth.' Many are invited, but few are chosen."

First Reading (Isa 25:6-10a)

On this mountain the LORD of hosts
    will provide for all peoples
a feast of rich food and choice wines,
    juicy, rich food and pure, choice wines.
On this mountain he will destroy
    the veil that veils all peoples,
the web that is woven over all nations;
    he will destroy death forever.

The Lord GOD will wipe away
    the tears from every face;
the reproach of his people he will remove
    from the whole earth; for the LORD has spoken.
    On that day it will be said:
"Behold our God, to whom we looked to save us!
    This is the LORD for whom we looked;
    let us rejoice and be glad that he has saved us!"
For the hand of the LORD will rest on this mountain.

Responsorial Psalm (Ps 23:1-3a, 3b-4, 5, 6)

R̸. (6cd) I shall live in the house of the Lord all the days of my life.

The LORD is my shepherd; I shall not want.
    In verdant pastures he gives me repose;
beside restful waters he leads me;
    he refreshes my soul.

R̸. I shall live in the house of the Lord all the days of my life.

He guides me in right paths
    for his name's sake.
Even though I walk in the dark valley
    I fear no evil; for you are at my side
with your rod and your staff
    that give me courage.

R̸. I shall live in the house of the Lord all the days of my life.

You spread the table before me
    in the sight of my foes;
you anoint my head with oil;
    my cup overflows.

R̸. I shall live in the house of the Lord all the days of my life.

Only goodness and kindness follow me
    all the days of my life;
and I shall dwell in the house of the LORD
    for years to come.

R̸. I shall live in the house of the Lord all the days of my life.

Second Reading (Phil 4:12-14, 19-20)

Reflecting on Living the Gospel

In a gospel story filled with such violence, it might be easy to forget we are dealing with a merciful God! As indicated in several parables, Matthew's church had the wisdom and experience to have learned that there were some in the church who did not belong. There are weeds within the wheat. Sadly, our modern experience reflects this too. Simply being in the church does not make one holy, God's chosen, or a paragon of virtue. Only God has the authority to eternally expel such a person. The sobering reminder that "many are invited but few are chosen" should cause us to pause, reflect, and reexamine our lives.

Connecting the Responsorial Psalm to the Readings

In today's psalm, God again is the host of a sumptuous banquet. The psalmist sings, "You spread a table before me / in the sight of my foes; / you anoint my head with oil; / my cup overflows." We see this imagery in the feast God invites all people to in the first reading and again in the banquet prepared by the king in Jesus' parable. The Bible often lifts up the virtue of hospitality. But it is important, too, to consider the duties expected of a guest. In the gospel parable the first set of guests ignore the invitation and refuse to attend. In contrast, not only does the psalmist gratefully sit at the table of the Lord, he also anticipates dwelling "in the house of the Lord for years to come."

Psalmist Preparation

How do you experience the abundant gifts of God in your own life?

Prayer

You have prepared a wedding banquet for your people, O God,
where all that has been broken may be joined by your saving love.
May we be ready to respond to your invitation.
I shall live in the house of the Lord
all the days of my life. Amen.

Gospel (Matt 22:15-21; L145A)

The Pharisees went off and plotted how they might entrap Jesus in speech. They sent their disciples to him, with the Herodians, saying, "Teacher, we know that you are a truthful man and that you teach the way of God in accordance with the truth. And you are not concerned with anyone's opinion, for you do not regard a person's status. Tell us, then, what is your opinion: Is it lawful to pay the census tax to Caesar or not?" Knowing their malice, Jesus said, "Why are you testing me, you hypocrites? Show me the coin that pays the census tax." Then they handed him the Roman coin. He said to them, "Whose image is this and whose inscription?" They replied, "Caesar's." At that he said to them, "Then repay to Caesar what belongs to Caesar and to God what belongs to God."

First Reading (Isa 45:1, 4-6)

Thus says the LORD to his anointed, Cyrus,
    whose right hand I grasp,
subduing nations before him,
    and making kings run in his service,
opening doors before him
    and leaving the gates unbarred:
For the sake of Jacob, my servant,
    of Israel, my chosen one,
I have called you by your name,
    giving you a title, though you knew me not.
I am the LORD and there is no other,
    there is no God besides me.
It is I who arm you, though you know me not,
    so that toward the rising and the setting of the sun
    people may know that there is none besides me.
I am the LORD, there is no other.

Responsorial Psalm (Ps 96:1, 3, 4-5, 7-8, 9-10)

R︎. (7b) Give the Lord glory and honor.

Sing to the LORD a new song;
    sing to the LORD, all you lands.
Tell his glory among the nations;
    among all peoples, his wondrous deeds.

R︎. Give the Lord glory and honor.

For great is the LORD and highly to be praised;
    awesome is he, beyond all gods.
For all the gods of the nations are things of nought,
    but the LORD made the heavens.

R︎. Give the Lord glory and honor.

Give to the LORD, you families of nations,
    give to the LORD glory and praise;
    give to the LORD the glory due his name!
Bring gifts, and enter his courts.

R︎. Give the Lord glory and honor.

Worship the LORD, in holy attire;
    tremble before him, all the earth;
say among the nations: The LORD is king,
    he governs the peoples with equity.

R︎. Give the Lord glory and honor.

Second Reading (1 Thess 1:1-5b)

Reflecting on Living the Gospel

In the modern, rather individualistic world in which we live, there is a temptation to believe that what we have, we have earned, a result of our own hard work or that of others, such as family. But today's gospel is a reminder that all we have is from God. As such, we should not be hoarders of God's good gifts. Even money itself should not be thought of as ours. Let us die to the notion of possessions, what is mine versus yours, and let us instead engage in a lifestyle of discipleship which shares what we have with the least among us.

TWENTY-NINTH SUNDAY IN ORDINARY TIME

Connecting the Responsorial Psalm to the Readings

Psalm 96 urges us to "[s]ing to the Lord a new song." This new song comes to life as the Israelites are freed from exile in Babylon and allowed to return to their homeland to begin the process of rebuilding and restoring what was lost.

Psalmist Preparation

Where is God calling you to embrace a new song in your life of faith?

Prayer

As your chosen people, Lord, you have made us citizens of heaven.
Help us reveal that your reign is here now
by giving you the rightful praise that belongs only to you.
Sing to the Lord a new song;
sing to the Lord, all you lands. Amen.

OCTOBER 25, 2020

Gospel (Matt 22:34-40; L148A)

When the Pharisees heard that Jesus had silenced the Sadducees, they gathered together, and one of them, a scholar of the law, tested him by asking, "Teacher, which commandment in the law is the greatest?" He said to him, "You shall love the Lord, your God, with all your heart, with all your soul, and with all your mind. This is the greatest and the first commandment. The second is like it: You shall love your neighbor as yourself. The whole law and the prophets depend on these two commandments."

First Reading (Exod 22:20-26)

Thus says the LORD:
"You shall not molest or oppress an alien,
　for you were once aliens yourselves in the land of Egypt.
You shall not wrong any widow or orphan.
If ever you wrong them and they cry out to me,
　I will surely hear their cry.
My wrath will flare up, and I will kill you with the sword;
　then your own wives will be widows, and your children orphans.

"If you lend money to one of your poor neighbors among my people,
　you shall not act like an extortioner toward him
　by demanding interest from him.
If you take your neighbor's cloak as a pledge,
　you shall return it to him before sunset;
　for this cloak of his is the only covering he has for his body.
What else has he to sleep in?
If he cries out to me, I will hear him; for I am compassionate."

Responsorial Psalm (Ps 18:2-3, 3-4, 47, 51)

℟. (2) I love you, Lord, my strength.

I love you, O LORD, my strength,
 O LORD, my rock, my fortress, my deliverer.

℟. I love you, Lord, my strength.

My God, my rock of refuge,
 my shield, the horn of my salvation, my stronghold!
Praised be the LORD, I exclaim,
 and I am safe from my enemies.

℟. I love you, Lord, my strength.

The LORD lives and blessed be my rock!
 Extolled be God my savior.
You who gave great victories to your king
 and showed kindness to your anointed.

℟. I love you, Lord, my strength.

Second Reading (1 Thess 1:5c-10)

Reflecting on Living the Gospel

We recall that Jesus' teachings were rooted in Mosaic Law and the prophets. Yet he emphasized or combined aspects of each that made them seem to come alive, or to be read and understood in a new way. It's certainly true that loving God and loving one's neighbor were commandments in Mosaic Law. But who had ever combined them like this before? All of our actions ought to flow from this twofold love. Loving God and loving neighbor go together, and they cannot be reduced one to the other or one over the other.

Connecting the Responsorial Psalm to the Readings

Today the psalmist praises God as his "strength," "rock," "fortress," "deliverer," and "stronghold." In giving us his summary of the law and the prophets in today's gospel reading, Jesus provides us with a firm foundation for faith. Earlier in the Gospel of Matthew, Jesus tells us, "Everyone who listens to these words of mine and acts on them will be like a wise man who built his house on rock" (Matt 7:24; NABRE). Despite the many questions and challenges that can arise in the life of discipleship, if we are actively loving God and loving our neighbor we know we are not being steered in the wrong direction.

Psalmist Preparation

How does your faith in God provide you with a firm foundation when faced with difficult decisions?

Prayer

Teach us, Lord, to imitate your Son, that we may love you
with all our heart, all our soul, and all our mind,
and love our neighbor as ourselves.
I love you, O Lord, my strength,
my rock, my fortress, my deliverer. Amen.

Gospel (Matt 5:1-12a; L667)

When Jesus saw the crowds, he
went up the mountain, and after
he had sat down, his disciples
came to him. He began to teach
them, saying:

"Blessed are the poor in spirit,
for theirs is the Kingdom of
heaven.
Blessed are they who mourn,
for they will be comforted.
Blessed are the meek,
for they will inherit the land.
Blessed are they who hunger and thirst for righteousness,
for they will be satisfied.
Blessed are the merciful,
for they will be shown mercy.
Blessed are the clean of heart,
for they will see God.
Blessed are the peacemakers,
for they will be called children of God.
Blessed are they who are persecuted for the sake of righteousness,
for theirs is the Kingdom of heaven.

Blessed are you when they insult you and persecute you and utter every
kind of evil against you falsely because of me. Rejoice and be glad, for
your reward will be great in heaven."

First Reading (Rev 7:2-4, 9-14)

I, John, saw another angel come up from the East, holding the seal of the
living God. He cried out in a loud voice to the four angels who were given
power to damage the land and the sea, "Do not damage the land or the
sea or the trees until we put the seal on the foreheads of the servants of
our God." I heard the number of those who had been marked with the
seal, one hundred and forty-four thousand marked from every tribe of
the children of Israel.

After this I had a vision of a great multitude, which no one could
count, from every nation, race, people, and tongue. They stood before the
throne and before the Lamb, wearing white robes and holding palm
branches in their hands. They cried out in a loud voice:

"Salvation comes from our God,
who is seated on the throne,
and from the Lamb."

All the angels stood around the throne and around the elders and the four living creatures. They prostrated themselves before the throne, worshiped God, and exclaimed:

"Amen. Blessing and glory, wisdom and thanksgiving,
honor, power, and might
be to our God forever and ever. Amen."

Then one of the elders spoke up and said to me, "Who are these wearing white robes, and where did they come from?" I said to him, "My lord, you are the one who knows." He said to me, "These are the ones who have survived the time of great distress; they have washed their robes and made them white in the Blood of the Lamb."

Responsorial Psalm (Ps 24:1-2, 3-4, 5-6)

℟. (cf. 6) Lord, this is the people that longs to see your face.

The LORD's are the earth and its fullness;
the world and those who dwell in it.
For he founded it upon the seas
and established it upon the rivers.

℟. Lord, this is the people that longs to see your face.

Who can ascend the mountain of the LORD?
or who may stand in his holy place?
One whose hands are sinless, whose heart is clean,
who desires not what is vain.

℟. Lord, this is the people that longs to see your face.

He shall receive a blessing from the LORD,
a reward from God his savior.
Such is the race that seeks for him,
that seeks the face of the God of Jacob.

℟. Lord, this is the people that longs to see your face.

See Appendix, p. 208, for Second Reading

Reflecting on Living the Gospel

As so many "official saints" have been priests, religious, and celibates, it's critically important that we have the words of the Beatitudes in today's gospel to remind us of what holiness looks like. Nowhere in the Beatitudes is there a word about celibacy. There is certainly nothing about one's vocational state (priest, sister, etc.). Instead, we have attributes such as "poor in spirit," "meek," and "merciful." These are the hallmarks of sanctity. And they can be practiced by anybody, religious or lay, Catholic or Protestant, even Christian or non-Christian. We recall that the Gospel of Matthew is much more about actions than words.

Connecting the Responsorial Psalm to the Readings

Today's psalm refrain connects us to the holy ones in heaven by our same desire to see the face of God. The middle verse asks, "Who can ascend the mountain of the Lord? / or who may stand in his holy place? / One whose hands are sinless, whose heart is clean, / who desires not what is in vain." In the Beatitudes, Jesus gives us the formula for this holiness that brings us close to God.

Psalmist Preparation

On the earth we find revelations of God's presence in creation, the people around us, the word of God, and the sacraments. Each nourishes our hunger for the living God, and yet, we long for the fullness of time when "we shall see him as he is," as the first letter of St. John tells us. In your own life of faith, how do you foster and live out this desire to see the face of God?

Prayer

With you, O God, we are never alone
for the saints walk with us.
May their example teach us what it means to be blessed.
Blessing and glory, wisdom and thanksgiving,
honor, power, and might be to our God forever and ever. Amen.

Gospel (Matt 25:1-13; L154A)

Jesus told his disciples this parable: "The kingdom of heaven will be like ten virgins who took their lamps and went out to meet the bridegroom. Five of them were foolish and five were wise. The foolish ones, when taking their lamps, brought no oil with them, but the wise brought flasks of oil with their lamps. Since the bridegroom was long delayed, they all became drowsy and fell asleep. At midnight, there was a cry,  'Behold, the bridegroom! Come out to meet him!' Then all those virgins got up and trimmed their lamps. The foolish ones said to the wise, 'Give us some of your oil, for our lamps are going out.' But the wise ones replied, 'No, for there may not be enough for us and you. Go instead to the merchants and buy some for yourselves.' While they went off to buy it, the bridegroom came and those who were ready went into the wedding feast with him. Then the door was locked. Afterwards the other virgins came and said, 'Lord, Lord, open the door for us!' But he said in reply, 'Amen, I say to you, I do not know you.' Therefore, stay awake, for you know neither the day nor the hour."

First Reading (Wis 6:12-16)

Resplendent and unfading is wisdom,
>   and she is readily perceived by those who love her,
>   and found by those who seek her.
She hastens to make herself known in anticipation of their desire;
>   whoever watches for her at dawn shall not be disappointed,
>   for he shall find her sitting by his gate.
For taking thought of wisdom is the perfection of prudence,
>   and whoever for her sake keeps vigil
>   shall quickly be free from care;
because she makes her own rounds, seeking those worthy of her,
>   and graciously appears to them in the ways,
>   and meets them with all solicitude.

Responsorial Psalm (Ps 63:2, 3-4, 5-6, 7-8)

℟. (2b) My soul is thirsting for you, O Lord my God.

O God, you are my God whom I seek;
   for you my flesh pines and my soul thirsts
   like the earth, parched, lifeless and without water.

℟. My soul is thirsting for you, O Lord my God.

Thus have I gazed toward you in the sanctuary
   to see your power and your glory,
for your kindness is a greater good than life;
   my lips shall glorify you.

℟. My soul is thirsting for you, O Lord my God.

Thus will I bless you while I live;
   lifting up my hands, I will call upon your name.
As with the riches of a banquet shall my soul be satisfied,
   and with exultant lips my mouth shall praise you.

℟. My soul is thirsting for you, O Lord my God.

I will remember you upon my couch,
   and through the night-watches I will meditate on you:
you are my help,
   and in the shadow of your wings I shout for joy.

℟. My soul is thirsting for you, O Lord my God.

Second Reading (1 Thess 4:13-18 [or 1 Thess 4:13-14])

Reflecting on Living the Gospel
The parable we read today should be a clarion call to "be prepared" for
the coming of Jesus at the end times. And even if we think the end times
are far, far away, my own personal end (death) may come when I least expect it. Am I prepared for that? Such a question can clarify our own priorities and behaviors. Jesus reminds us that the fools are the ones who
were not prepared for the coming of the master. Let us be like the wise
ones, attentive to the coming of the Lord, for we know not when that day
might be.

Connecting the Responsorial Psalm to the Readings

In today's responsorial psalm we find images of seeking and keeping vigil. The psalmist sings, "O God, you are my God whom I seek" and "through the night-watches I will meditate on you." Thirst for the living God motivates the psalmist's ardent searching and patient waiting. No ordinary thirst, this spiritual need is "like the earth, parched, lifeless and without water."

Psalmist Preparation

When in your life have you experienced this depth of thirst for God? In the spiritual life, we are to cultivate the longing for God as well as to find the sources that truly quench our desire. Only God can fill the ache within, and so, like the psalmist, we are content to search and wait for him to reveal himself.

Prayer

Those who keep watch for you, O God, will never be disappointed.
Focus our gaze that we may be awake and ready to see you
where others fail to recognize your presence.
Thus will I bless you while I live;
my lips will call upon your name. Amen.

Gospel (Matt 25:14-30 [or Matt 25:14-15, 19-21]; L157A)

Jesus told his disciples this parable:

"A man going on a journey called in his servants and entrusted his possessions to them. To one he gave five talents; to another, two; to a third, one— to each according to his ability. Then he went away. Immediately the one who received five talents went and

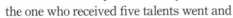
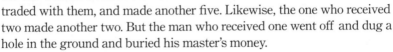

traded with them, and made another five. Likewise, the one who received two made another two. But the man who received one went off and dug a hole in the ground and buried his master's money.

"After a long time the master of those servants came back and settled accounts with them. The one who had received five talents came forward bringing the additional five. He said, 'Master, you gave me five talents. See, I have made five more.' His master said to him, 'Well done, my good and faithful servant. Since you were faithful in small matters, I will give you great responsibilities. Come, share your master's joy.' Then the one who had received two talents also came forward and said, 'Master, you gave me two talents. See, I have made two more.' His master said to him, 'Well done, my good and faithful servant. Since you were faithful in small matters, I will give you great responsibilities. Come, share your master's joy.' Then the one who had received the one talent came forward and said, 'Master, I knew you were a demanding person, harvesting where you did not plant and gathering where you did not scatter; so out of fear I went off and buried your talent in the ground. Here it is back.' His master said to him in reply, 'You wicked, lazy servant! So you knew that I harvest where I did not plant and gather where I did not scatter? Should you not then have put my money in the bank so that I could have got it back with interest on my return? Now then! Take the talent from him and give it to the one with ten. For to everyone who has, more will be given and he will grow rich; but from the one who has not, even what he has will be taken away. And throw this useless servant into the darkness outside, where there will be wailing and grinding of teeth.'"

First Reading (Prov 31:10-13, 19-20, 30-31)

When one finds a worthy wife,
  her value is far beyond pearls.
Her husband, entrusting his heart to her,
  has an unfailing prize.
She brings him good, and not evil,
  all the days of her life.
She obtains wool and flax
  and works with loving hands.
She puts her hands to the distaff,
  and her fingers ply the spindle.
She reaches out her hands to the poor,
  and extends her arms to the needy.
Charm is deceptive and beauty fleeting;
  the woman who fears the LORD is to be praised.
Give her a reward for her labors,
  and let her works praise her at the city gates.

Responsorial Psalm (Ps 128:1-2, 3, 4-5)

R℣. (cf. 1a) Blessed are those who fear the Lord.

Blessed are you who fear the LORD,
  who walk in his ways!
For you shall eat the fruit of your handiwork;
  blessed shall you be, and favored.

R℣. Blessed are those who fear the Lord.

Your wife shall be like a fruitful vine
  in the recesses of your home;
your children like olive plants
  around your table.

R℣. Blessed are those who fear the Lord.

Behold, thus is the man blessed
  who fears the LORD.
The LORD bless you from Zion:
  may you see the prosperity of Jerusalem
  all the days of your life.

R℣. Blessed are those who fear the Lord.

Second Reading (1 Thess 5:1-6)

Reflecting on Living the Gospel

Today's parable can move us to action, investing ourselves more fully in the Christian life. And for the Gospel of Matthew that means service of others, especially the less fortunate. Though there can be freeloaders, contributing little to no effort of their own, the parable today reminds us that there will come a time when God will take stock of each person's efforts. May this gospel motivate us to continue serving without counting the cost, investing fully of ourselves and our talents. When there is an accounting, we want to hear the words, "Come, share your master's joy."

Connecting the Responsorial Psalm to the Readings

Today's psalm refrain proclaims, "Blessed are those who fear the Lord." In some ways this can seem contrary to the gospel, where the servant given one talent goes and buries it "out of fear." God does not desire that we fear him in a way that paralyzes us from taking risks and using the gifts we have been given. The term "fear of the Lord" in the Bible is also sometimes translated as having "wonder and awe in the Lord's presence." Instead of paralyzing us, this wonder and awe can draw us forward with delight to seek to serve God in all we do.

Psalmist Preparation

How do you experience wonder and awe in God's presence?

Prayer

You have blessed us, Lord, with the desire to serve you.
May we use the gifts you entrust to us for the glory of your name,
for our good and the good of all your holy church.
Blessed are those who fear the Lord,
who walk in God's ways. Amen.

Gospel (Matt 25:31-46; L160A)

Jesus said to his disciples: "When the Son of Man comes in his glory, and all the angels with him, he will sit upon his glorious throne, and all the nations will be assembled before him. And he will separate them one from another, as a shepherd separates the sheep from the goats. He will place the sheep on his right and the goats on his left. Then the king will say to those on his right, 'Come, you who are blessed by  my Father. Inherit the kingdom prepared for you from the foundation of the world. For I was hungry and you gave me food, I was thirsty and you gave me drink, a stranger and you welcomed me, naked and you clothed me, ill and you cared for me, in prison and you visited me.' Then the righteous will answer him and say, 'Lord, when did we see you hungry and feed you, or thirsty and give you drink? When did we see you a stranger and welcome you, or naked and clothe you? When did we see you ill or in prison, and visit you?' And the king will say to them in reply, 'Amen, I say to you, whatever you did for one of the least brothers of mine, you did for me.' Then he will say to those on his left, 'Depart from me, you accursed, into the eternal fire prepared for the devil and his angels. For I was hungry and you gave me no food, I was thirsty and you gave me no drink, a stranger and you gave me no welcome, naked and you gave me no clothing, ill and in prison, and you did not care for me.' Then they will answer and say, 'Lord, when did we see you hungry or thirsty or a stranger or naked or ill or in prison, and not minister to your needs?' He will answer them, 'Amen, I say to you, what you did not do for one of these least ones, you did not do for me.' And these will go off to eternal punishment, but the righteous to eternal life."

First Reading (Ezek 34:11-12, 15-17)

Thus says the Lord GOD:
   I myself will look after and tend my sheep.
As a shepherd tends his flock
   when he finds himself among his scattered sheep,
   so will I tend my sheep.

I will rescue them from every place where they were scattered
    when it was cloudy and dark.
I myself will pasture my sheep;
    I myself will give them rest, says the Lord GOD.
The lost I will seek out,
    the strayed I will bring back,
    the injured I will bind up,
    the sick I will heal,
    but the sleek and the strong I will destroy,
    shepherding them rightly.

As for you, my sheep, says the Lord GOD,
    I will judge between one sheep and another,
    between rams and goats.

Responsorial Psalm (Ps 23:1-2, 2-3, 5-6)

℟. (1) The Lord is my shepherd; there is nothing I shall want.

The LORD is my shepherd; I shall not want.
    In verdant pastures he gives me repose.

℟. The Lord is my shepherd; there is nothing I shall want.

Beside restful waters he leads me;
    he refreshes my soul.
He guides me in right paths
    for his name's sake.

℟. The Lord is my shepherd; there is nothing I shall want.

You spread the table before me
    in the sight of my foes;
you anoint my head with oil;
    my cup overflows.

℟. The Lord is my shepherd; there is nothing I shall want.

Only goodness and kindness follow me
    all the days of my life;
and I shall dwell in the house of the LORD
    for years to come.

℟. The Lord is my shepherd; there is nothing I shall want.

See Appendix, p. 208, for Second Reading

Reflecting on Living the Gospel

It is a bold thing to identify with Christ. Self-sacrifice, love of the other, and service are central to the identity of a Christian. How mortally dangerous it is, then, to call oneself Christian, to claim the role of disciple, without performing the required actions. It would be better not to claim the title at all. The will of God is caring for the poor and for the stranger. These are not merely kind acts, but the basis of salvation, for Christian and non-Christian alike. Let us keep before us the awesome call and responsibility to express our faith in action, not merely words.

Connecting the Responsorial Psalm to the Readings

Once again our psalm for today is Psalm 23. This is the third time this psalm has been proclaimed at the liturgy in the past two months. We prayed with it on the Twenty-Eighth Sunday in Ordinary Time, as well as on All Souls' Day. It is fitting for today, given the "sheep" present in both the first reading and the gospel; it is particularly hearkening to the reading from Ezekiel in which God proclaims that he will be the one to tend the scattered sheep of the house of Israel. Our psalm reminds us that with the Lord as our shepherd, we will dwell in security and safety. This psalm could also be seen as another model for how we are to care for others. In John's gospel Jesus tells his disciples, "As I have loved you, so you also should love one another" (13:34; NABRE). Psalm 23 gives us a portrait of Jesus, the Good Shepherd, who guides his sheep and abundantly fulfills their needs. This is the generosity that we are to emulate in serving others.

Psalmist Preparation

Just as the Lord shepherds you, how do you seek to be a good shepherd for those who have been given into your care?

Prayer

At the end of our days, Lord, you will ask not what we have accomplished
but whom we have loved and served.
May we be among those welcomed into your kingdom.
Only goodness and kindness follow me
all the days of my life. Amen.

FIRST SUNDAY OF ADVENT, December 1, 2019
Second Reading (Rom 13:11-14)
Brothers and sisters: You know the time; it is the hour now for you to awake from sleep. For our salvation is nearer now than when we first believed; the night is advanced, the day is at hand. Let us then throw off the works of darkness and put on the armor of light; let us conduct ourselves properly as in the day, not in orgies and drunkenness, not in promiscuity and lust, not in rivalry and jealousy. But put on the Lord Jesus Christ, and make no provision for the desires of the flesh.

SECOND SUNDAY OF ADVENT, December 8, 2019
Second Reading (Rom 15:4-9)
Brothers and sisters: Whatever was written previously was written for our instruction, that by endurance and by the encouragement of the Scriptures we might have hope. May the God of endurance and encouragement grant you to think in harmony with one another, in keeping with Christ Jesus, that with one accord you may with one voice glorify the God and Father of our Lord Jesus Christ.

Welcome one another, then, as Christ welcomed you, for the glory of God. For I say that Christ became a minister of the circumcised to show God's truthfulness, to confirm the promises to the patriarchs, but so that the Gentiles might glorify God for his mercy. As it is written:

Therefore, I will praise you among the Gentiles
and sing praises to your name.

THE IMMACULATE CONCEPTION OF THE BLESSED VIRGIN MARY, December 9, 2019
Second Reading (Eph 1:3-6, 11-12)
Brothers and sisters: Blessed be the God and Father of our Lord Jesus Christ, who has blessed us in Christ with every spiritual blessing in the heavens, as he chose us in him, before the foundation of the world, to be holy and without blemish before him. In love he destined us for adoption to himself through Jesus Christ, in accord with the favor of his will, for the praise of the glory of his grace that he granted us in the beloved.

In him we were also chosen, destined in accord with the purpose of the One who accomplishes all things according to the intention of his will, so that we might exist for the praise of his glory, we who first hoped in Christ.

THIRD SUNDAY OF ADVENT, December 15, 2019
Second Reading (Jas 5:7-10)
Be patient, brothers and sisters, until the coming of the Lord. See how the farmer waits for the precious fruit of the earth, being patient with it until it receives the early and the late rains. You too must be patient. Make your hearts firm, because the coming of the Lord is at hand. Do not complain, brothers and sisters, about one another, that you may not be judged. Behold, the Judge is standing before the gates. Take as an example of hardship and patience, brothers and sisters, the prophets who spoke in the name of the Lord.

FOURTH SUNDAY OF ADVENT, December 22, 2019
Second Reading **(Rom 1:1-7)**

Paul, a slave of Christ Jesus, called to be an apostle and set apart for the gospel of God, which he promised previously through his prophets in the holy Scriptures, the gospel about his Son, descended from David according to the flesh, but established as Son of God in power according to the Spirit of holiness through resurrection from the dead, Jesus Christ our Lord. Through him we have received the grace of apostleship, to bring about the obedience of faith, for the sake of his name, among all the Gentiles, among whom are you also, who are called to belong to Jesus Christ; to all the beloved of God in Rome, called to be holy. Grace to you and peace from God our Father and the Lord Jesus Christ.

THE NATIVITY OF THE LORD, *Vigil Mass*, December 25, 2019
Second Reading **(Acts 13:16-17, 22-25)**

When Paul reached Antioch in Pisidia and entered the synagogue, he stood up, motioned with his hand, and said, "Fellow Israelites and you others who are God-fearing, listen. The God of this people Israel chose our ancestors and exalted the people during their sojourn in the land of Egypt. With uplifted arm he led them out of it. Then he removed Saul and raised up David as king; of him he testified, 'I have found David, son of Jesse, a man after my own heart; he will carry out my every wish.' From this man's descendants God, according to his promise, has brought to Israel a savior, Jesus. John heralded his coming by proclaiming a baptism of repentance to all the people of Israel; and as John was completing his course, he would say, 'What do you suppose that I am? I am not he. Behold, one is coming after me; I am not worthy to unfasten the sandals of his feet.'"

THE NATIVITY OF THE LORD, *Mass at Midnight*, December 25, 2019
Second Reading **(Titus 2:11-14)**

Beloved: The grace of God has appeared, saving all and training us to reject godless ways and worldly desires and to live temperately, justly, and devoutly in this age, as we await the blessed hope, the appearance of the glory of our great God and savior Jesus Christ, who gave himself for us to deliver us from all lawlessness and to cleanse for himself a people as his own, eager to do what is good.

THE NATIVITY OF THE LORD, *Mass at Dawn*, December 25, 2019
Second Reading **(Titus 3:4-7)**

Beloved:
When the kindness and generous love
    of God our savior appeared,
not because of any righteous deeds we had done
    but because of his mercy,
he saved us through the bath of rebirth
    and renewal by the Holy Spirit,
whom he richly poured out on us
    through Jesus Christ our savior,
so that we might be justified by his grace
    and become heirs in hope of eternal life.

THE NATIVITY OF THE LORD, *Mass During the Day,*
December 25, 2019
Second Reading (Heb 1:1-6)

Brothers and sisters: In times past, God spoke in partial and various ways to our ancestors through the prophets; in these last days, he has spoken to us through the Son, whom he made heir of all things and through whom he created the universe,

who is the refulgence of his glory, the very imprint of his being,
and who sustains all things by his mighty word.
When he had accomplished purification from sins,
he took his seat at the right hand of the Majesty on high,
as far superior to the angels
as the name he has inherited is more excellent than theirs.

For to which of the angels did God ever say:

You are my son; this day I have begotten you?

Or again:

I will be a father to him, and he shall be a son to me?

And again, when he leads the firstborn into the world, he says:

Let all the angels of God worship him.

THE HOLY FAMILY OF JESUS, MARY, AND JOSEPH, December 29, 2019
Second Reading (Col 3:12-21 [or Col 3:12-17])

Brothers and sisters: Put on, as God's chosen ones, holy and beloved, heartfelt compassion, kindness, humility, gentleness, and patience, bearing with one another and forgiving one another, if one has a grievance against another; as the Lord has forgiven you, so must you also do. And over all these put on love, that is, the bond of perfection. And let the peace of Christ control your hearts, the peace into which you were also called in one body. And be thankful. Let the word of Christ dwell in you richly, as in all wisdom you teach and admonish one another, singing psalms, hymns, and spiritual songs with gratitude in your hearts to God. And whatever you do, in word or in deed, do everything in the name of the Lord Jesus, giving thanks to God the Father through him.

Wives, be subordinate to your husbands, as is proper in the Lord. Husbands, love your wives, and avoid any bitterness toward them. Children, obey your parents in everything, for this is pleasing to the Lord. Fathers, do not provoke your children, so they may not become discouraged.

THE SOLEMNITY OF THE BLESSED VIRGIN MARY, MOTHER OF GOD,
January 1, 2020
Second Reading (Gal 4:4-7)

Brothers and sisters: When the fullness of time had come, God sent his Son, born of a woman, born under the law, to ransom those under the law, so that we might receive adoption as sons. As proof that you are sons, God sent the Spirit of his Son into our hearts, crying out, "Abba, Father!" So you are no longer a slave but a son, and if a son then also an heir, through God.

THE EPIPHANY OF THE LORD, January 5, 2020
Second Reading (Eph 3:2-3a, 5-6)

Brothers and sisters: You have heard of the stewardship of God's grace that was given to me for your benefit, namely, that the mystery was made known to me by revelation. It was not made known to people in other generations as it has now been revealed to his holy apostles and prophets by the Spirit: that the Gentiles are coheirs, members of the same body, and copartners in the promise in Christ Jesus through the gospel.

THE BAPTISM OF THE LORD, January 12, 2020
Second Reading (Acts 10:34-38)

Peter proceeded to speak to those gathered in the house of Cornelius, saying: "In truth, I see that God shows no partiality. Rather, in every nation whoever fears him and acts uprightly is acceptable to him. You know the word that he sent to the Israelites as he proclaimed peace through Jesus Christ, who is Lord of all, what has happened all over Judea, beginning in Galilee after the baptism that John preached, how God anointed Jesus of Nazareth with the Holy Spirit and power. He went about doing good and healing all those oppressed by the devil, for God was with him."

ASH WEDNESDAY, February 26, 2020
Second Reading (2 Cor 5:20–6:2)

Brothers and sisters: We are ambassadors for Christ, as if God were appealing through us. We implore you on behalf of Christ, be reconciled to God. For our sake he made him to be sin who did not know sin, so that we might become the righteousness of God in him.

Working together, then, we appeal to you not to receive the grace of God in vain. For he says:

In an acceptable time I heard you,
and on the day of salvation I helped you.

Behold, now is a very acceptable time; behold, now is the day of salvation.

FIRST SUNDAY OF LENT, March 1, 2020
Second Reading (Rom 5:12-19 [or Rom 5:12, 17-19])

Brothers and sisters: Through one man sin entered the world, and through sin, death, and thus death came to all men, inasmuch as all sinned— for up to the time of the law, sin was in the world, though sin is not accounted when there is no law. But death reigned from Adam to Moses, even over those who did not sin after the pattern of the trespass of Adam, who is the type of the one who was to come.

But the gift is not like the transgression. For if by the transgression of the one, the many died, how much more did the grace of God and the gracious gift of the one man Jesus Christ overflow for the many. And the gift is not like the result of the one who sinned. For after one sin there was the judgment that brought condemnation; but the gift, after many transgressions, brought acquittal. For if, by the transgression of the one, death came to reign through that one, how much more will those who receive the abundance of grace and of the gift of justification come to reign in life through the one Jesus Christ. In conclusion, just as through one transgression condemnation came upon all, so, through one righteous act, acquittal and life came to all. For just as through the disobedience of the one man the many were made sinners, so, through the obedience of the one, the many will be made righteous.

SECOND SUNDAY OF LENT, March 8, 2020
Second Reading (2 Tim 1:8b-10)

Beloved: Bear your share of hardship for the gospel with the strength that comes from God.

He saved us and called us to a holy life, not according to our works but according to his own design and the grace bestowed on us in Christ Jesus before time began, but now made manifest through the appearance of our savior Christ Jesus, who destroyed death and brought life and immortality to light through the gospel.

THIRD SUNDAY OF LENT, March 15, 2020
Second Reading (Rom 5:1-2, 5-8)

Brothers and sisters: Since we have been justified by faith, we have peace with God through our Lord Jesus Christ, through whom we have gained access by faith to this grace in which we stand, and we boast in hope of the glory of God.

And hope does not disappoint, because the love of God has been poured out into our hearts through the Holy Spirit who has been given to us. For Christ, while we were still helpless, died at the appointed time for the ungodly. Indeed, only with difficulty does one die for a just person, though perhaps for a good person one might even find courage to die. But God proves his love for us in that while we were still sinners Christ died for us.

FOURTH SUNDAY OF LENT, March 22, 2020
Second Reading (Eph 5:8-14)

Brothers and sisters: You were once darkness, but now you are light in the Lord. Live as children of light, for light produces every kind of goodness and righteousness and truth. Try to learn what is pleasing to the Lord. Take no part in the fruitless works of darkness; rather expose them, for it is shameful even to mention the things done by them in secret; but everything exposed by the light becomes visible, for everything that becomes visible is light. Therefore, it says: / "Awake, O sleeper, / and arise from the dead, / and Christ will give you light."

FIFTH SUNDAY OF LENT, March 29, 2020
Second Reading (Rom 8:8-11)

Brothers and sisters: Those who are in the flesh cannot please God. But you are not in the flesh; on the contrary, you are in the spirit, if only the Spirit of God dwells in you. Whoever does not have the Spirit of Christ does not belong to him. But if Christ is in you, although the body is dead because of sin, the spirit is alive because of righteousness. If the Spirit of the One who raised Jesus from the dead dwells in you, the One who raised Christ from the dead will give life to your mortal bodies also, through his Spirit dwelling in you.

PALM SUNDAY OF THE LORD'S PASSION, April 5, 2020
Second Reading (Phil 2:6-11)

Christ Jesus, though he was in the form of God,
    did not regard equality with God
    something to be grasped.
Rather, he emptied himself,
    taking the form of a slave,
    coming in human likeness;
    and found human in appearance,

he humbled himself,
becoming obedient to the point of death,
even death on a cross.
Because of this, God greatly exalted him
and bestowed on him the name
which is above every name,
that at the name of Jesus
every knee should bend,
of those in heaven and on earth and under the earth,
and every tongue confess that
Jesus Christ is Lord,
to the glory of God the Father.

HOLY THURSDAY EVENING MASS OF THE LORD'S SUPPER, April 9, 2020
Second Reading (1 Cor 11:23-26)
Brothers and sisters: I received from the Lord what I also handed on to you, that the Lord Jesus, on the night he was handed over, took bread, and, after he had given thanks, broke it and said, "This is my body that is for you. Do this in remembrance of me." In the same way also the cup, after supper, saying, "This cup is the new covenant in my blood. Do this, as often as you drink it, in remembrance of me." For as often as you eat this bread and drink the cup, you proclaim the death of the Lord until he comes.

GOOD FRIDAY OF THE LORD'S PASSION, April 10, 2020
Second Reading (Heb 4:14-16; 5:7-9)
Brothers and sisters: Since we have a great high priest who has passed through the heavens, Jesus, the Son of God, let us hold fast to our confession. For we do not have a high priest who is unable to sympathize with our weaknesses, but one who has similarly been tested in every way, yet without sin. So let us confidently approach the throne of grace to receive mercy and to find grace for timely help.

In the days when Christ was in the flesh, he offered prayers and supplications with loud cries and tears to the one who was able to save him from death, and he was heard because of his reverence. Son though he was, he learned obedience from what he suffered; and when he was made perfect, he became the source of eternal salvation for all who obey him.

EASTER SUNDAY, April 12, 2020
Second Reading (1 Cor 5:6b-8 or [Col 3:1-4])
Brothers and sisters: Do you not know that a little yeast leavens all the dough? Clear out the old yeast, so that you may become a fresh batch of dough, inasmuch as you are unleavened. For our paschal lamb, Christ, has been sacrificed. Therefore, let us celebrate the feast, not with the old yeast, the yeast of malice and wickedness, but with the unleavened bread of sincerity and truth.

SECOND SUNDAY OF EASTER, April 19, 2020
Second Reading (1 Pet 1:3-9)
Blessed be the God and Father of our Lord Jesus Christ, who in his great mercy gave us a new birth to a living hope through the resurrection of Jesus Christ from the dead, to an inheritance that is imperishable, undefiled, and unfading, kept in

heaven for you who by the power of God are safeguarded through faith, to a salvation that is ready to be revealed in the final time. In this you rejoice, although now for a little while you may have to suffer through various trials, so that the genuineness of your faith, more precious than gold that is perishable even though tested by fire, may prove to be for praise, glory, and honor at the revelation of Jesus Christ. Although you have not seen him you love him; even though you do not see him now yet believe in him, you rejoice with an indescribable and glorious joy, as you attain the goal of your faith, the salvation of your souls.

THIRD SUNDAY OF EASTER, April 26, 2020
Second Reading (1 Pet 1:17-21)
Beloved: If you invoke as Father him who judges impartially according to each one's works, conduct yourselves with reverence during the time of your sojourning, realizing that you were ransomed from your futile conduct, handed on by your ancestors, not with perishable things like silver or gold but with the precious blood of Christ as of a spotless unblemished lamb.

He was known before the foundation of the world but revealed in the final time for you, who through him believe in God who raised him from the dead and gave him glory, so that your faith and hope are in God.

FOURTH SUNDAY OF EASTER, May 3, 2020
Second Reading (1 Pet 2:20b-25)
Beloved: If you are patient when you suffer for doing what is good, this is a grace before God. For to this you have been called, because Christ also suffered for you, leaving you an example that you should follow in his footsteps.

He committed no sin, and no deceit was found in his mouth.

When he was insulted, he returned no insult; when he suffered, he did not threaten; instead, he handed himself over to the one who judges justly. He himself bore our sins in his body upon the cross, so that, free from sin, we might live for righteousness. By his wounds you have been healed. For you had gone astray like sheep, but you have now returned to the shepherd and guardian of your souls.

FIFTH SUNDAY OF EASTER, May 10, 2020
Second Reading (1 Pet 2:4-9)
Beloved: Come to him, a living stone, rejected by human beings but chosen and precious in the sight of God, and, like living stones, let yourselves be built into a spiritual house to be a holy priesthood to offer spiritual sacrifices acceptable to God through Jesus Christ. For it says in Scripture:

Behold, I am laying a stone in Zion,
a cornerstone, chosen and precious,
and whoever believes in it shall not be put to shame.

Therefore, its value is for you who have faith, but for those without faith:

The stone that the builders rejected
has become the cornerstone,

and

A stone that will make people stumble,
and a rock that will make them fall.

They stumble by disobeying the word, as is their destiny.

You are "a chosen race, a royal priesthood, a holy nation, a people of his own, so that you may announce the praises" of him who called you out of darkness into his wonderful light.

SIXTH SUNDAY OF EASTER, May 17, 2020
Second Reading (1 Pet 3:15-18)
Beloved: Sanctify Christ as Lord in your hearts. Always be ready to give an explanation to anyone who asks you for a reason for your hope, but do it with gentleness and reverence, keeping your conscience clear, so that, when you are maligned, those who defame your good conduct in Christ may themselves be put to shame. For it is better to suffer for doing good, if that be the will of God, than for doing evil. For Christ also suffered for sins once, the righteous for the sake of the unrighteous, that he might lead you to God. Put to death in the flesh, he was brought to life in the Spirit.

THE ASCENSION OF THE LORD, May 21 or 24, 2020
Second Reading (Eph 1:17-23)
Brothers and sisters: May the God of our Lord Jesus Christ, the Father of glory, give you a Spirit of wisdom and revelation resulting in knowledge of him. May the eyes of your hearts be enlightened, that you may know what is the hope that belongs to his call, what are the riches of glory in his inheritance among the holy ones, and what is the surpassing greatness of his power for us who believe, in accord with the exercise of his great might, which he worked in Christ, raising him from the dead and seating him at his right hand in the heavens, far above every principality, authority, power, and dominion, and every name that is named not only in this age but also in the one to come. And he put all things beneath his feet and gave him as head over all things to the church, which is his body, the fullness of the one who fills all things in every way.

SEVENTH SUNDAY OF EASTER, May 24, 2020
Second Reading (1 Pet 4:13-16)
Beloved: Rejoice to the extent that you share in the sufferings of Christ, so that when his glory is revealed you may also rejoice exultantly. If you are insulted for the name of Christ, blessed are you, for the Spirit of glory and of God rests upon you. But let no one among you be made to suffer as a murderer, a thief, an evildoer, or as an intriguer. But whoever is made to suffer as a Christian should not be ashamed but glorify God because of the name.

PENTECOST, May 31, 2020
Second Reading (1 Cor 12:3b-7, 12-13)
Brothers and sisters: No one can say, "Jesus is Lord," except by the Holy Spirit.

There are different kinds of spiritual gifts but the same Spirit; there are different forms of service but the same Lord; there are different workings but the same God who produces all of them in everyone. To each individual the manifestation of the Spirit is given for some benefit.

As a body is one though it has many parts, and all the parts of the body, though many, are one body, so also Christ. For in one Spirit we were all baptized into one body, whether Jews or Greeks, slaves or free persons, and we were all given to drink of one Spirit.

THE MOST HOLY TRINITY, June 7, 2020
Second Reading (2 Cor 13:11-13)
Brothers and sisters, rejoice. Mend your ways, encourage one another, agree with one another, live in peace, and the God of love and peace will be with you. Greet one another with a holy kiss. All the holy ones greet you.

The grace of the Lord Jesus Christ and the love of God and the fellowship of the Holy Spirit be with all of you.

THE MOST HOLY BODY AND BLOOD OF CHRIST, June 14, 2020
Second Reading (1 Cor 10:16-17)
Brothers and sisters: The cup of blessing that we bless, is it not a participation in the blood of Christ? The bread that we break, is it not a participation in the body of Christ? Because the loaf of bread is one, we, though many, are one body, for we all partake of the one loaf.

THE ASSUMPTION OF THE BLESSED VIRGIN MARY, August 15, 2020
Second Reading (1 Cor 15:20-27)
Brothers and sisters: Christ has been raised from the dead, the firstfruits of those who have fallen asleep. For since death came through man, the resurrection of the dead came also through man. For just as in Adam all die, so too in Christ shall all be brought to life, but each one in proper order: Christ the firstfruits; then, at his coming, those who belong to Christ; then comes the end, when he hands over the Kingdom to his God and Father, when he has destroyed every sovereignty and every authority and power. For he must reign until he has put all his enemies under his feet. The last enemy to be destroyed is death, for "he subjected everything under his feet."

ALL SAINTS, November 1, 2020
Second Reading (1 John 3:1-3)
Beloved: See what love the Father has bestowed on us that we may be called the children of God. Yet so we are. The reason the world does not know us is that it did not know him. Beloved, we are God's children now; what we shall be has not yet been revealed. We do know that when it is revealed we shall be like him, for we shall see him as he is. Everyone who has this hope based on him makes himself pure, as he is pure.

THE SOLEMNITY OF OUR LORD JESUS CHRIST THE KING, November 22, 2020
Second Reading (1 Cor 15:20-26, 28)
Brothers and sisters: Christ has been raised from the dead, the firstfruits of those who have fallen asleep. For since death came through man, the resurrection of the dead came also through man. For just as in Adam all die, so too in Christ shall all be brought to life, but each one in proper order: Christ the firstfruits; then, at his coming, those who belong to Christ; then comes the end, when he hands over the kingdom to his God and Father, when he has destroyed every sovereignty and every authority and power. For he must reign until he has put all his enemies under his feet. The last enemy to be destroyed is death. When everything is subjected to him, then the Son himself will also be subjected to the one who subjected everything to him, so that God may be all in all.